WORKING
with
TEENAGERS
The essential handbook

NICK AIKEN
**with contributions by Geoff Willis,
Mike King and Edward Bonner**

New Revised Edition

MarshallPickering
An Imprint of HarperCollinsPublishers

Marshall Pickering is an Imprint of
HarperCollins*Religious*
Part of HarperCollins*Publishers*
77–85 Fulham Palace Road, London W6 8JB

First published in Great Britain
in 1994 by Marshall Pickering

1 3 5 7 9 10 8 6 4 2

A catalogue record for this book is
available from the British Library

ISBN 0 551 02817 3

Printed and bound in Great Britain by
HarperCollinsManufacturing Glasgow

CONTENTS

This book is dedicated to all those
who are seeking to bring young people into
a knowledge of our risen and living Saviour

To God be praise

ACKNOWLEDGEMENTS

I have so many people to thank who have helped in the writing of this book. In particular I am thankful to the great many young people whom it has been a joy and a privilege to be able to encourage in their Christian faith. I feel confident that they will continue to grow in Christ and prove to be a shining light to others.

There are also the friends who have helped and advised in the work that has gone into this book. I would like to express especial thanks to Tim and Margaret Dean, John Miller, Christine White, Paul Hooper, Mark Ashton, Juli Wills, David Holt, Gordon Kegg, Keith Smalldon, Robin Elks, Kevin Scott, John Broughall, Kevin McGarahan, Simon Parish, Paul Barber and Tony Chanter.

I should like also to acknowledge the help given by 'Signpost' which was devised by the National Youth Office with the assistance of the Anglican DYO network, and to express my appreciation of the information provided in the 'Youth Work Pack' produced by the Church of England Youth Services, and to Graham Richards.

I am grateful to Edward Bonner, Mike King and Geoff Willis who have made their own particular contribution to this book on the subjects in which they have a great deal of knowledge and experience.

To my colleagues in The Education Centre at Guildford Cathedral for all their support and friendship, thanks.

Nick Aiken

PREFACE TO THE NEW EDITION

When I began as Youth officer for the Diocese of Guildford in 1986 the first thing that struck me was the lack of resources for youth work. Mark Ashton from CYFA and Steve Chalke from the Baptist Church, had just written two very good books, but apart from that there was nothing fresh or new that was effectively helping youth leaders in a practical way. It was at this point that Marshall Pickering asked me if I would write a handbook for leaders that would complement what was already written. Hence after many, many hours of labour *Working with Teenagers* was published in 1988. The book, I'm pleased to say, had a large number of extremely favourable reviews in all the major Christian papers. This was followed by excellent sales of many thousands. I find it particularly pleasing to think that this book has helped so many youth leaders all over the country.

Working with Teenagers has continued to be very much in demand and so we felt it was time to revise and update some of the material, so that the book would continue to be of value to a youth leader in the 90s.

The youth scene has undergone many changes since the late 80s. A lot of those changes are very positive. The amount of books and resources available to youth leaders has mushroomed. This can only be good news for the hard-pressed leaders desperate to find something that will help them put across the Gospel message in an attractive and helpful manner. But the important thing to remember with any resource, however good it may be, is to adapt it. You should always adapt any material to the needs of your group if it is to work effectively.

Another very important change is that youth work has a far higher priority in the church's life. The reasons for this are numerous. God has been renewing His Church and giving us a greater awareness of the need to communicate the Gospel to the future generations. Adults are beginning to realise that young people's work is crucial, and teenagers need to be spiritually challenged and encouraged into an active membership of God's Church. The profile and importance of youth work has been raised by many faithful Christians who have been working away at both a national and a local level. That work was given a real boost when George Carey was made Archbishop. Dr Carey has shown a tremendous support for youth work and is someone who realises the critical importance of work among the young. I'm sure that with his encouragement youth work will continue to assume a higher priority in the Church in the future. I personally am grateful for the support and participation Dr Carey gave to 'Eagle's Wings' the national training event for the Church of England, which I organised with various other Diocesan Youth Officers.

It is probably worth remembering that the Church, and by that I mean all the churches in Britain, is in fact working among more teenagers than any other organisation in the country. If you add together all the youth activities that go on you would find that more young people go to church youth activities than to anything else. If you add to this the often open door that exists with all the uniformed organisations, it encourages you away from the usual despair at the lack of the Church's impact into being encouraged to face the future with renewed hope.

However it is important as we head towards the end of this millennium, and with statistics showing the large number of young people leaving the Church, that we double our efforts to reach the young people of today with the Good News of God's Love.

I wish you all of God's grace as you seek to bring His love to the young people of today.

Nick Aiken   August 1993

PART ONE

The Church and Young People

1
AIMS OF YOUTH WORK

Every work must have an aim. If it does not then it will eventually falter and fall apart.

In this opening chapter I want to deal with what I think should be the fundamental aim of Church-based youth work – the aim which should underlie all other aims and objectives that we may set ourselves in dealing with young people.

Let's start at the end: the end, that is, of Matthew's Gospel. Jesus, before His ascension, gave parting instructions to the disciples: 'All authority in heaven and on earth has been given to me. Go therefore and make disciples of all nations . . .' (Matthew 28:18 & 19). With those words of command, confident of the presence of the Living Christ with them and renewed by the power of the Holy Spirit at Pentecost, they went out and did just that. But the command of Christ is implicit for all disciples to go and do the same. If we as Christians fail to nurture our young people to follow the Master, we will have failed both God and our young people, and fallen short in our own Christian calling. Mark Ashton, in his book *Christian Youth Work*, has said that 'The first aim of Christian youth work must be to present a young person with the claims of Jesus Christ'.

We must show our young people that God has a claim on their lives, and for those who are prepared to accept that claim we must provide the right environment where they can grow as followers of Christ. A youth group has to have its aims and emphasis firmly based on the Christian faith, and then work from that basis.

Some youth leaders and churches attempt to provide a social

activity for teenagers and then introduce a bit of Christianity into the programme in a vain hope that it may have some effect. It very rarely, if ever, works. Unless the group starts from a Christian basis and expresses that by nurturing the youth in the life of discipleship, it will never achieve what must be its fundamental aim.

Our aim is evangelism and the nurture of young disciples. What does that mean? Again let us return to the words of Jesus. In Matthew 10:24 & 25, Jesus is recorded as saying: 'A disciple is not above his teacher, nor a servant above his master; it is enough for the disciple to be like his teacher, and the servant like his master.'

The goal that we have as Christians and the goal we should set before our young people is to be like Jesus. St Bernard of Clairvaux said, 'What we love we shall grow to resemble'. Christ is the one who is not just our example but also our inspiration. This means that we need to teach our young people who Jesus is. They, as well as ourselves, need to have a clear understanding of who Christ was, His life and teaching, and also who He is today. One helpful piece of advice that I am sure many of my contemporaries were given when *we* were teenagers was 'In whatever circumstances you find yourself if confronted by a difficult situation, always ask what would Jesus do – and then do it'. However, the one weakness in this piece of very good advice is that you have to know enough about the character and person of Christ before it is possible to live our your discipleship in that way. So, if we and our teenagers are going to be disciples, we have got to know who the Master is in order to be able to imitate Him. St Paul said: 'Be imitators of me, as I am of Christ' (1 Corinthians 11:1).

At the heart of the life of any disciple should be the power of God's love. The greatest goal we can set ourselves and our young people is the call to fulfil what Jesus described as the Greatest Commandment: 'You shall love the Lord your God with all your heart, and with all your soul, and with all your mind. This is the great and first commandment' (Matthew 22:37 & 38).

4

God demands from us all of our love simply because He has given us all of *His* love. It is a love of sacrifice and of relationship. It is a love that makes the greatest demands upon us and which is jealous and not prepared to accept any rivals. This is why Jesus threw down a challenge to anyone who wanted to be His disciple – namely, that it would involve all their love as well as the very best of that love. When Jesus said, 'If anyone comes to me and does not hate his own father and mother and wife and children and brothers and sisters, yes, even his own life, he cannot be my disciple' (Luke 14:26), He was highlighting in a very dramatic way that compromise is not possible. God demands of us our first allegiance. That is the message we ourselves need to take to heart and which we should put before our teenagers. Clive Andrews, in his book *Handbook of Parish Youth Work*, says that 'The ultimate aim of Christian youth work of whatever kind is to proclaim the gospel . . .'. Indeed, that is right, but we must face up to the fact that the gospel involves asking people to make a sacrifice of themselves.

Another important dimension in the life of discipleship is obedience. It is very tempting, among young people as well as adults, to lay great emphasis on spiritual experiences. Teenagers are particularly prone to this because they are at a time in their lives when they are influenced by emotional highs. The impression can often be that feelings are important in judging your own relationship with God. If you are feeling good and God is close, then that is a test of how your Christian life is going. However, we need to be mindful of Jesus' words in John 8:31 – 'If you continue in my word you are truly my disciples . . .' The heart of the life of discipleship comes back to obedience to the words of Christ. Often the young people who are still on the path of faith many years after leaving the youth group are not the ones who were always to the forefront of the group claiming great experiences, but rather those who quietly took a back seat and actually got on with putting their discipleship into action.

The great theologian Hans Kung said that to be a Christian

is to be truly human. We have got to let our young people see that obedience to Christ's teachings is in fact the most natural and normal thing for us, because it is He who reveals the Father and thereby shows us the way in which God the Creator wants us to live our lives.

Another aspect of the central aim of creating and nurturing young disciples is that we should expect to see some evidence and testimony of a change in quality of life. Jesus said, 'By this my Father is glorified, that you bear much fruit, and so prove to be my disciples' (John 15:8). A disciple is someone who should bear fruit: the fruit of the Spirit.

I was recently with a youth leader who told me the story of a young girl who had become a Christian. What had happened was that one of the members of the youth group had invited her along to a social evening they were having. The girl at first was a little apprehensive but when she arrived she was very struck by everyone's warmth and friendliness to her. She found it quite remarkable and decided to come again. After a few months, by which time she had got to know the group, she decided to go along to one of their Bible study groups. This was a big step for her because she did not come from a Christian family and they never went to church. After a few weeks of attending the Bible-study group, her interest in spiritual things had grown and she decided to come to church. Well, it was not too long before she became a Christian, and what had essentially attracted her was the friendliness of the Christian teenagers in the group.

The fruit of the Spirit and of Christian living is described in Galatians 5:22 – 'But the fruit of the Spirit is love, joy, peace, patience, kindness, goodness, faithfulness, gentleness, self-control; against such there is no law.' In many ways this describes what should be the hallmark of any gathering of Christians of whatever age. These should be the expressions of our individual and corporate discipleship. It is very humbling when you see a group of teenagers setting themselves these goals for living and then watch them putting them into action.

6

As one poster I have seen exclaimed: 'God is looking for spiritual fruit, not religious nuts.'

Finally, the life of discipleship is a life of action. It is fascinating to see how Jesus trained His followers. He first of all provided the model and example, and then told the twelve to go and live and do the same. When Jesus sent out the disciples on their first assignment, He gave them a pretty demanding task. Just take a look at Matthew 10:7 & 8 – 'and preach as you go saying, The Kingdom of God is at hand. Heal the sick, raise the dead, cleanse lepers, cast out demons.'

One may feel that Christ was being more than a little unreasonable; however, He was merely instructing them to do what He Himself was doing. Jesus had shown what He expected a disciple of His to do and so that is the model they followed. After His resurrection the early Christians did the same thing. The challenge is therefore on us to encourage the gifts of the Holy Spirit not only within our own lives but also in the lives of our young people. One youth group I visited asked me to talk on God the Holy Spirit. When I asked them during the course of the address if any of them prayed in tongues, I drew a blank stare. No one had told them that a disciple of Christ should expect to see the gifts of the Spirit, both natural and supernatural, operating within their lives. By contrast, the members of another group who had been taught about this aspect of our spiritual heritage were actively open to what God may do through the power of the Holy Spirit. One particular evening the leader felt it was right to stop and wait on God. His hunch was right because four of the young people were, in the silence, given a vision or prophetic word which they shared with the group. All the teenagers that evening went home greatly encouraged and particularly aware that God had been in their presence. It can sometimes be the case that the young are very much open to God because they are so eager to grow and learn and discover the new things that God is doing.

So what should be our basic aim in working with young people? To challenge them with the message of Christ and to nurture them in the way of Christian discipleship.

SETTING AIMS, OBJECTIVES AND GOALS

Questions to be discussed either between you, the youth leader and your clergy or within your youth committee – you may find it helpful to put your results down on paper.

1 What are the aims of your youth group?
2 What are the aims which you consider are of central importance?
3 How are your aims reflected in the objectives that you have set the group?
4 How are you fulfilling your objectives?
5 What goals do you have for the group – for the next 6 months, 12 months and three years?

SUGGESTIONS FOR FURTHER READING

Clive Andrews, *Handbook of Parish Youth Work* (Mowbray).

Mark Ashton, *Christian Youth Work* (Kingsway Publications).

Phil Moon, *Young People and the Bible* (Marshall Pickering).

Derek Prime, *Directions for Christian Living* (Marshall Pickering).

Jim Wallis, *Agenda for Biblical People* (Triangle).

Pete Ward, *Youth Culture and the Gospel* (Marshall Pickering).

M. Warren, *Youth and the Future of the Church: Ministry with Youth and Young Adults* (Winston Press).

David Watson, *Discipleship* (Hodder and Stoughton).

—, *One in the Spirit* (Hodder and Stoughton).

2
THE YOUTH LEADER

We have looked at what should be the basic aim of Christian youth work and in the next chapter we shall look at leadership skills. But what about *you*, the youth leader? Why are you a youth leader? Probably for the majority of us it's because the vicar or pastor asked us if we would either lead or help to lead the group. Why?! Because we would be very good at it; and besides there is no one else to do it.

I got involved in Church youth work by accident; it was certainly not by intention. In my final year at theological college I received a 'phone call from the rector of a large and active parish south of London. Actually, I'd never heard of the place and after he had put the 'phone down I went to look for a map to find out where the parish was. Anyway, he invited me down for a weekend to look at the parish and this obviously gave him the opportunity to figure out whether I would be any good at the job. On the Sunday I attended the various morning services at the parish and daughter church. I felt very attracted to the rector and the people. The worship had great variety. One service had been a Sung Eucharist with plenty of colour and drama, though no 'smells and bells', the other a very dignified Prayer Book Matins. Over lunch we had the opportunity to talk some more and I increasingly felt drawn to come to the parish. Then the rector said, 'Of course, if you come to this parish we would expect you to lead the teenage youth group.' Well, in my usual cavalier fashion I said, 'Sure, no problem.'

That night I was taken along to the evening service. It was a fairly traditional Prayer Book experience with a good positive atmosphere. I noticed that this was the service that most of the young people came to. They all sat together on the right-hand side of the church. Safety in numbers, I suppose! There seemed an awful lot of them, but mind you, the service was pretty well-attended anyway. After the service finished I was taken along to the youth group, and that was when my earlier confidence fell apart. In the hall there were around seventy teenagers in various states of hyperactivity. Most of them seemed to be overcompensating for the previous hour of subdued reflection.

Before I was able to put my exit plan into action, I was introduced to the assistant leaders and told to sit down. As the leader who was speaking that evening endeavoured to silence the group, he announced that the subject for discussion was 'Christianity and Rock Music'. I breathed a sigh of relief. At least I had heard of Genesis and I occasionally watched Top of the Pops. However, 95 per cent of the groups they mentioned I had never heard of, and the line of discussion seemed a little alien to the intellectual arguments I was used to with Biblical criticism. How I wished I hadn't skipped that lecture at college on 'Christianity and modern culture'!

When the evening ended I made my way back to the rectory in a state of shock. I thought the only thing I can do is to tell the truth. 'Richard', I said, 'I've got to be honest with you. I haven't got a clue how to run a youth group. In fact, before tonight I'd never been to a youth group in my life!' Thrusting a cup of coffee into my hand, the rector exclaimed: 'Don't worry! You'll be great; just get on with it.' That was my introduction to youth work.

But what about *you*, the youth leader? Well, you'll be glad to know that it really doesn't matter what you look like or what age you are. One of your primary qualifications should be that you actually have a love and concern for the young people. Some of the best youth leaders I know are well into middle age and lost their hair years ago. Male leaders I'm referring to, of course! Also you do not have to be anything but yourself. If you try to be anything else the teenagers will see through it instantly. Trying to be trendy is a sure recipe for disaster. Young people do not expect and usually do not want leaders to be like them.

What are some of the other ingredients of a youth leader?

You have got to be prepared to make a sacrifice. The Christian life is a path of self-denial, and the sacrifice of time, energy and emotion is part of that. There will be, at times, a conflict of interests where the youth group or individuals within it will take precedence over other items that will also demand time and emotion. Time and time again in the Church I see that what is needed more than money is Christians who are prepared to sacrifice themselves, to give and to reach out to young people. Here it may be appropriate for you to relinquish other responsibilities. Far-sighted clergy and church councils who ask people to take on responsibility for the youth often absolve them of other duties and committees.

Part of the preparedness to make a sacrifice is also that of being ready to give and to serve. Again, this is at the very heart of the Christian Gospel and the life of discipleship. We are called to give all of ourselves to God and to give of ourselves in love to those around us. Here the words of Jesus are again very powerful: 'It is more blessed to give than to receive' (Acts 20:35).

The sad thing is that we in the Church of God seem to have corporately lost this vision that Christ gave us. The Church is not seen to be the servant of people bringing its light and life. Yet this was the example that Christ challenged us with – 'For the Son of man also came not to be served but to serve, and to give his life as a ransom for many' (Mark 10:45). A youth leader should be prepared to serve the young people for whom he has responsibility. That service will be a whole mixture of fun, frustration, satisfaction, agony, joy and exhaustion.

There also is a very dangerous strand of thought prevalent in much of the Church that runs something like this – unless I am being well taught in my faith and well-equipped through the Church's teaching ministry, then I cannot exercise any

11

ministry of my own. What this means in practical terms is that too many Christians have their eyes focused on what they receive. They look at their own spiritual need and refuse to do anything until their own needs are met. This attitude, which is widespread, is not only dangerous but insidious, since it often goes under the guise of virtuous spirituality. Yet it is in giving that we receive, it is in teaching that we are taught. A youth leader, or indeed any Christian, should not construe his or her own spiritual needs as an excuse not to give to others. There are too many spiritually obese Christians who have their eyes focused on themselves and not on God and the needs of others around them.

Even the best and most experienced youth leaders will find themselves in situations where they feel unable to cope and are spiritually unprepared. But in each situation we find ourselves in, however well or badly equipped, we are called to serve and minister to others.

Another aspect of our role should be a desire to see the young come to a maturity of person and of faith. The real joy of working with young people is seeing them grow up – seeing them realise their potential as individuals. It is a great privilege to get alongside them and share with them and see them grow. It is always a great source of amusement to show old photos or slides of past camps and house parties. You see John or Lucy who joined your group at the age of thirteen or fourteen. At the time maybe they were either quiet or loud and difficult and did not play much of an active part. Now at eighteen they have grown up, their personalities have developed and they are showing a real beauty of character. Possibly now they have various gifts of vitality and enthusiasm which they bring to the group and they are an influence for good. With some of those young people you may have shared a lot. Jacky's mother may have died of cancer, Jim's father may have left home for another woman. You have been with them in their times of worry about exams; and you have experienced with them the joys of camp weeks or house parties. It's all an incredible privilege to be part of another person's world and to assist in a small way in his or her physical and spiritual growth.

Christian youth leaders should themselves be alive to God and have a sense of urgency and expectation about what they are doing. If we are thrilled about what God has done and are looking to Him in anticipation of what He is going to do, then that sense of expectation will positively communicate itself to the young people. If we have allowed God to get hold of us and fill us with His Holy Spirit, then the power and vibrancy of God will overflow to others. As Mark Ashton has pointed out: 'Sometimes it's not the Gospel that is being rejected but the class, educational and cultural overtones that we have laid upon it.' When young people are brought to see that Christianity is not the cold dusty religion they thought it to be, but a vitally real relationship with the living God, then they respond to the one who has attracted millions to Himself to worship and follow Him.

The satisfaction of being a youth leader is rarely through instant results. For sure, there may be instances of dramatic responses to God, but these will be rare; with most it will mean the slow and gentle nurture in the faith. The seeds which are well-rooted will be those that are sown over a long period of time and grow gradually. At first you may see only a little fruit in individual lives. Probably because of time, the majority of young people with whom you are dealing will show very little evidence of a deep, mature and powerful faith. The real value of what you have done may, in fact, only show itself five, ten, twenty or thirty years later. Some will continue to grow and in their late twenties take up full-time Christian work. Some in their thirties may take up responsibilities in their church as warden, housegroup leader, Sunday school teacher. And so it goes on.

Some youth groups may grow up and be big and dynamic, but the real value of what has been done by you the leader will show itself more significantly when they have left you and moved on. It is very easy to have groups which spring up in a great flurry of activity yet quickly die away because, at heart, it was all froth and no substance. Besides, it is not numbers that are important or the activity but the quality of the love and relationship that is present. Jesus only had twelve disciples, so be careful not to judge your success by the numbers that turn up.

A youth leader should be open to new ideas and should make full use of the human and physical resources available. The job is one of creating the most out of the potential of any group, so that at all levels there is change, development and growth. A good leader will also be on the look-out to encourage the development of leadership in others so that the focus of the group is not solely around the present leadership. This is also important for the purely practical reason that you need to train up those who will replace you when you leave.

At this point it is probably worth stopping and thinking about the implications of what has been said and their practical outworkings for you before you move on to the next chapter.

3
LEADERSHIP SKILLS

Well now – we have looked at the youth leader and thought a little about his or her personal situation. Let's now look at the area of leadership skills.

Most of us probably have a picture in our mind of the ideal youth leader. That image may be a reflection of the person who ran the youth club when we were young and who may well have had a particular influence on us. Or the picture perhaps derives from our admiration for a friend who runs a group – someone who is omni-talented, good looking, younger than us, better educated, playing the guitar with great skill, excellent at speaking and leading discussion groups, and with a wonderful Christian faith. If you have a friend who is that kind of 'ideal' youth leader, then it can be pretty depressing – especially when you compare yourself to him or her. But don't be intimidated by others and your impression of them, because your skills and gifts are just as vital and important as theirs. And whatever you are doing, it will be a valid contribution to the situation you are in and the service you are offering.

Part of our problem is that we often suffer from hang-ups about the ideal leader. The image of the 'hero' can be very strong. But in reality we do not really want or need heroes when it comes to working with young people from a Christian perspective. Heroes can, in fact, do a great deal of damage because their success is often more apparent than real. The young may become too dependent on the personality of the leader, and this can often be a block to their seeing a way through to a personal faith of their own. The hero-figure is often not the most stable of characters; moreover, a group dominated by such a figure may all too easily collapse when that kind of leader goes away from it, because it has not been given enough life and responsibility of its own. The best leaders are not the hero-figures but rather those who encourage the gifts and talents of the young people themselves.

I came across this observation recently which I think conveys very well the essence of leadership skills:

As for the best leaders, the people hardly notice their
  existence.
The next best they honour,
The next best they dislike.
But when the best leaders work is done, the people say
  'We did it ourselves'.

Some folk say that leaders are born, and doubtless there are those for whom leadership skills come very easily. But for most of us it is a question of identifying our skills and through experience letting them develop.

SOME CRUCIAL AREAS OF LEADERSHIP

Communication

There is, in fact, a whole section on communcication skills in this handbook (see chapter 13, below). But it is important, at this stage, to stress that you need to be a good communicator. Irrespective of what you are trying to communicate, skill in getting people clearly to understand your words and purpose is of vital importance – and this applies equally whether you are seeking to convey a spiritual truth or to discipline someone in your group. All too often the Church fails to get across its message because it fails to communicate.

Communication has a lot to do with identifying and understanding the culture and thought-forms that young people are part of. If they can see that you are aware of and understand the things that affect them and they feel concerned about, this has a powerful effect on drawing you nearer to them. This is closely linked with the whole business of awareness.

Sensitivity is a crucial part of this skill because it involves listening not only to what the young are saying but also to what they are feeling. A sensitive youth leader will have so much to offer through being someone teenagers can approach without feeling judged or threatened.

Communication is probably more about listening than about talking. How much time do you feel you spend listening to young people?

Motivation

Being able to motivate and encourage others is another important leadership skill. The people you are seeking to motivate will be the other youth leaders and particularly the teenagers themselves. This skill is very demanding, especially when you go through the black periods in groups or fellowships when the young people are negative and critical of what is happening. Often it is just a phase that they go through which may last a few weeks or a few months. Their motivation to attend and take part in the group hits a low. The only thing to do in that sort of situation is to persevere.

In many ways it comes back to your own motivation. If you are motivated to turn up on time, contribute your best to the evening, make an effort to talk to people and show that you believe what you are doing is important, then it has an effect on others. Your example will be an inspiration to the rest. Part also of this is to think and act positively. As has been said:

Positive Attitudes = Positive Results
Negative Attitudes = Negative Results
No Thoughts   = No Results!!

If you hope to motivate your fellow leaders and young people, you need to be able to encourage their gifts and positive attributes. At a very basic level it may be just a question of saying thank-you and showing your appreciation for something they have done. So often a lot of people's gifts lie dormant because others have not taken the trouble to express their gratitude for something that has been done well. Such lack of appreciation curbs any growth and fails to allow someone to develop confidence in God-given gifts and abilities. A good leader should be able to spot the potential in others and then be prepared to take calculated risks in giving greater responsibility to those who are showing promise in particular areas.

Evaluation

All leaders need, at some stage, to evaluate what they individually are doing and also how the group is corporately developing. A lot of evaluation will be going on, on a weekly basis. You will be judging how well an event was planned, organised and executed. Without calling it evaluation, you will be making a value judgement on probably all the occasions that you meet together. A skilful leader should be able to see clearly what has happened, not just on an organisational level but also on the level of personal and spiritual dynamics.

Let's consider evaluation in just two areas.

1 *Personal evaluation as to how you are developing as a youth leader.* This would be best discussed with your clergy and with your fellow leaders if you have any. But you may wish to go one step further than that, to gain a clear idea of how you are coming across to the group of teenagers. This evaluation activity may deepen your relationship with the young people, but it takes a lot of ego strength and a willingness to accept criticism. This is how to do it. Explain to them that you want an honest evaluation of your qualities as a youth leader. Ask them to mark these on a scale of one to ten, starting with ten as the highest. Some of the qualities could be:

- explains the Bible clearly;
- has time for me;
- understands me;
- helps me to understand God;

- is a good worship leader;
- is like Jesus;
- answers my questions;
- is an interesting teacher;
- listens;
- is easy to talk to;
- is a Christian example;
- shows me how to live for God.

It is probably best not to discuss what people feel but collect the lists together – unsigned, of course – and take them home. Don't go through them that night, because you will be tired; but sometime during the next few days examine them with a trusted friend, and then go out afterwards and do something you enjoy.

2 *The area of group evaluation.* In fact, most of the chapters of this book involve evaluation of different kinds in a whole variety of areas. But here I just want us to think of assessing how the group is going.

Again, give each member of the group a pen or pencil. Here are some of the questions you may wish to put to them:

- I come to the group because . . .
- The best thing about the group is . . .
- The worst thing about the group is . . .
- One thing I've learnt about God from this group is . . .
- One thing I've learnt about relationships with others is . . .
- I wish the group was more . . .
- One thing I wish the group could do is . . .
- I wish the group would stop doing . . .

The findings are best discussed with the other leaders or assistant leaders. You will have to separate the legitimate critics from those who are just moaning. When you have discussed thoroughly the findings, decide on what plan of action you are going to employ to strengthen what you are doing. Then – and this is of great importance – pray for the group as a whole and the individuals in it.

19

Developing leadership skills

None of us would think of going to a doctor who had done no training, or consult a lawyer who had no qualifications. So, therefore, we owe it to ourselves and our young people to take whatever opportunities are available for training as a youth leader. The effect of good training should be to heighten our awareness of our own gifts and skills. It should also help to stimulate our understanding of new areas of leadership of which we may not be aware.

There are a number of opportunities available for those not just beginning youth work but who would value 'in-service' training. The following list of contacts indicates some of the sources, appropriate to different denominational and worshipping traditions, for information and advice on training in leadership skills.

- The Diocesan Youth Officer in your own diocese.
- The Methodist Association of Youth Clubs.
- The United Reformed Churches Youth Training Officer
- Headquarters Organisation of your own Denomination.
- The Church Youth Fellowship Association.
- Scripture Union.
- British Youth for Christ.
  (For address of the above, see the Appendix of National Addresses, below.)
- The County Youth Officer in your own area.
- 'Brainstormers', sponsored by *Youthwork and Alpha* Magazine, 37 Elm Road, New Malden, Surrey KT3 3HB.
- 'Eagle's Wings' run by the Church of England Youth Services. Contact the National Youth Office at Church House, Westminster, London SW1P 3NZ.

SUGGESTIONS FOR FURTHER READING

E.R. Dayton and T.W. Engstrom, *Strategy for Leadership* (Marc Europe).

John Perry, *Effective Christian Leadership* (Hodder and Stoughton).

Philip Greenslade, *Learning to Lead* (Marshall Pickering).

Chua Wee Hian, *Learning to Lead* (I.V.P.).

Philip King, *Leadership Explosion* (Hodder and Stoughton).

Youth Work Pack. Diocese of York, available from the Rectory, Leconfield, Beverley HU17 7NP.

4

SUPPORT AND INTEGRATION

This is a subject that arouses strong feelings among a lot of youth leaders. Many feel they do not get the support and encouragement they need from their clergy and congregation. A sense of isolation is common among Church youth leaders and is also prevalent in the secular County youth service. Often the leader finds himself caught between the group and the congregation, particularly when something goes wrong or when an item is broken. It seems that some congregations only voice any comment about the youth work that is going on when it is to complain and criticise. There is usually no lack of those who will tell you how you should be doing your job, and it is often those who don't even know the teenagers within their church community. If you are not in this situation from time to time, then count yourself fortunate; but what lies at the heart of this issue is something which should concern every youth leader: integration with the church.

Some groups end up as para-church movements; here there is very little contact between the group and the church and its members. In extreme cases this is disastrous because part of the aim of every youth leader should be to see the young people grow up into regular worship in their church.

How, then, do you foster integration with the rest of the congregation of which the young people are part? The short answer is − by a lot of hard work and a diversity of means.

In the first place, it is important to let the church know what the group is doing. Good communication is at the heart of good relationships and dispels so much misunderstanding. Make regular or at least occasional reports to your PCC, church council or group of elders. This is usually the key decision-making body, and its members have an important role within the church. They decide on church policy and financial matters, both of which are areas which will affect the youth group. They also invariably reflect the weight of feeling and opinions within the congregation, so it is important that they are aware and well-informed of what the teenagers are doing. If people do not know what is happening, they cannot take any interest in what is going on and give it their support. A good youth leader needs to have his eye on PR.

There are many other ways to communicate the activities of the youth and encourage general support. Keep your clergy well-informed. A good pastor will have more than just a passing interest in the youth side of the congregation. But not all clergy are perfect and most are extremely busy people involved in so many different areas. It is easy for them to overlook the work you are doing, so it is important that you arrange to liaise with them from time to time. You should inform him or her not only of the group's actual activities, but also about the pastoral and spiritual needs of individuals in the group. Your clergy will be able to give you advice and, through their links in other areas, particularly with parents, they may be aware of issues which can be of help to you in understanding a problem an individual may have. Your clergy should be a source of support but they can only be so if they are aware of what your needs are, individually and as a group. Also, meeting with them should be an opportunity to pray and commend to God the lives of those who are so precious to Him.

Many churches have a weekly news-sheet. It may be a good idea to use this tool as a means of informing the congregation of what is going on. From time to time an article in the parish magazine can be included about a recent special event that the group was involved in. You may wish to write the article yourself or get one of the young people to do it. However, if you do ask one of the teenagers, make sure you take a careful look at the article before it goes to press. A couple of years ago I made the mistake of asking two fourteen-year-olds to

write an item for the magazine about the Confirmation weekend
I took them on – they were part of a group from our parish
of about seventy candidates and leaders who went to
Ashburnham Place in Sussex. It was a great event, tending to
be rather noisy, with so many young people present. During
a wide game which we played on the Sunday, the annual
tradition of throwing the curate into the lake was observed.
The only problem was that, on this occasion, the teenagers
threw each other in as well. In the minds of the two fourteen-
year-olds, all the Bible-study and discussion groups got lost
amidst their impressions and most of their article highlighted
the fun and games they had got up to. When the article
appeared in the parish magazine containing vivid descriptions
of the lake exploits, it all sounded like an excursion by St
Trinian's. I thought to myself, 'Oh dear, there's going to be
trouble,' and sure enough there was. For three months letters
appeared in the magazine, but that was only a token problem
compared with the endless explaining I had to do to concerned
older members of the church. So take care!

Another dimension that helps in the business of
communication is that of serving. A youth group should be
able to serve the rest of the congregation in a whole variety
of ways. Sadly, as I have previously said, the whole notion
of genuine service to others seems to have got a bit lost in the
Church today. Too much focus often falls on individuals and
heroes. But the example of Jesus is crucial. 'The Son of Man
came not to be served but to serve' (Mark 10:45). Your young
people can serve the younger children in the church (and
especially) the elderly. Jobs such as gardening, painting,
shopping and various odd-jobs can do so much to bring the
family of God closer together. Recently a youth leader got a
letter from an elderly widow in the parish asking for some help
in painting the walls of her living room. She explained that
she could not move except with the aid of her Zimmer and
could not afford to pay a professional painter. When the leader
read out the letter to the group that Sunday night, he was
surprised to get offers of help from two rather vivacious girls

whom he thought to be the least practically minded members of the group. A few weeks later he asked them how they had got on. They remarked 'fine'. He thought no more of the event until a most beautiful letter appeared in the church magazine written by this elderly lady. She described in most glowing terms how kind and warm these two young girls had been. She was so moved that she wanted the whole church community to know how impressed she was with the young.

The point is that, as Christians, we should not serve others for the praise or reward we may get, but if people can see the good and positive side of the young it helps overcome any alienation that may be prevalent.

It may also be appropriate from time to time to have an open-evening. You could make it an event to which you specifically invite either the whole congregation or your young people's parents. Parents are often very grateful to youth leaders for what they are doing, and appreciate the contact and gaining of greater understanding of what the group's activities are and what you are trying to achieve. With careful planning on how you wish to run the occasion and what type of presentation you want to give, you can do a great deal in fostering closer relationships.

Finally, in this area of your specific responsibilities as a leader, make sure the congregation are aware of the prayer needs of the young people. In most churches intercessory prayer takes place, either in the formal service or at prayer meetings. If the group is supported by people's prayers, that is something of crucial value in its own right, but it also helps people grow in care and concern for those for whom they are praying.

The whole area of integration with the rest of the body of the church is vital, not just because of the support the older members should be giving to the leader and the young, but because the young have so much to contribute to the life and worship of the congregation. Pope John Paul II recognised this when he said recently in an address:

Dear young people, to bring to the world the joyful news of the Gospel, the Church needs your enthusiasm and your generosity. You know, it can happen that your elders, after the difficult journey and the trials they have undergone fall prey to fear or weariness and let the dynamism which is the mark of every Christian vocation grow weak. It can also happen that institutions, because of routine or deficiencies of their members, are not sufficiently at the service of the Gospel message. Because of this the Church needs the witness of your hope and your zeal in order to fulfil her mission better.

And he went on to say: 'The Church needs your presence and your participation.'

Since our young people are part of the body of Christ, our identity should always be with the whole people of God gathered together in the one congregation. If we see ourselves as independent in our life, worship and use of God's gifts, then our theology and practice will be fundamentally flawed. St Paul encourages us by saying (Ephesians 4:3-6):

> Be eager to maintain the unity of the Spirit in the bond of peace. There is one body and one Spirit, just as you were called to the one hope that belongs to your call, one Lord, one faith, one baptism, one God and Father of us all, who is above all and through all and in all.

The goal of any youth group should be to express our profound unity that we have in Christ with those who are also called into the new life. St Paul finishes his words on body theology in Ephesians by stating, in the second part of verse 16 in chapter 4, that the whole body 'when each part is working properly, makes bodily growth and upbuilds itself in love'.

If the youth group's integration with the rest of the congregation is inadequate, then the life of the whole church community will be inadequate. It is, however, inspiring to see churches where our unity in Christ is being expressed within the whole family age-group of the congregation. This not only stands as a testimony to the outside world but enables the body to grow in love for God and each member as all share together in worship. When you see God using the younger members of the family to express the gifts of the Holy Spirit to the whole body, you realise afresh how Our Father seeks to draw us closer together.

So it is of utmost importance that we encourage our youth to play as full a part as possible with the on-going life of our local church. Encourage them to take part in the service – to lead the prayers, to read the lessons, to act as a steward or sidesperson. Stop and think for a moment about all the activities within the life of the church and how much part the young people play in them. Are they part of the choir? You may be fortunate and have a joint male and female choir. What about the music group or drama and dance group, if you have one? Some of the best dance groups have a complete cross-section of ages. In many churches the teenagers play a very important role in the Sunday School programme and derive a great deal of pleasure and satisfaction from being involved. In one church I visited it was both amusing and encouraging to see three of the older teenagers, who were all distinctly well-built 'macho' rugby players, working in the Sunday School for 5–7 year olds. The children thought they were wonderful and the three boys had apparently been trying to persuade their other friends to join in as well.

The young should, wherever possible, be taking part in church life at every level in its worship, its activities and decision-making.

Starting from the support available from the home church, it is important to make full use of the channels of help available at local and national level. Meeting together with other leaders from the area, either from your own denomination or ecumenically, has value not only in exchanging ideas but also in sharing successes and failures, and providing mutual support. Do you know who are the other youth leaders? Are there any ventures which you might consider planning together? Often one youth group will plan an event which could benefit the members of another group, particularly if it is a smaller one.

Yet because the channels of communication are poor, other folk do not get to hear of it, and an opportunity is missed. Do you know the other leaders in your deanery, district or denominational structure?

Apart from the support available at a local level, there are the full-time officers employed by the Church who should be made full use of. Each diocese usually has a lay or ordained Youth Officer, and each denominational area will have its own full-time workers. They can provide a lot of help, support and training.

At the national level there are a number of organisations which seek to assist youth workers. Some of these are listed in the Appendix of National Addresses at the end of this book. They can supply many useful items of materials for a whole range of activities and interests, and often also speakers. In addition – and as we noted in chapter 3 – they have their own system of training schemes.

Support is also available through the County Youth Service, with its trained youth workers. Most areas will have a local club or office. Generally, the Youth Service personnel have a lot of sympathy and admiration for what the Church is doing and are more than willing to lend their support. It is worth finding out where your local office is. This can be done through your Diocesan Youth Officer or by contacting your County Council. Frequently Youth Officers are able to make various facilities available to groups, and you will probably find their personal and practical support very helpful. It is certainly worth liaising with your local officer.

In short, no leader should feel that he or she is not getting the support that is needed.

5
TEACHING

One of the primary roles of a leader is to be a teacher. Christ taught His disciples and in the Great Commission in Matthew 28:20 authorised their mission to all peoples everywhere to 'teach them to observe all that I have commanded you'. A youth leader within the context of his church and youth group should be part of a community which is growing in its understanding and knowledge of God. St Paul in Ephesians encourages us to be no longer like children and he goes on to say in 4:15 – 'Rather, speaking the truth in love, we are to grow up in every way into Him who is the head, into Christ . . .' The hallmark of a child of God is of someone who is growing and learning. Teaching needs to be a central part of the group to aid this growing process.

But the model of teaching we have is of a blackboard, chalk and a classroom, with someone standing up at the front, talking. Possibly if we used the word 'teaching' with our young people, it would create all sorts of misconceptions. With a number of youth groups I know, if you mention having a Bible study or doing anything of an overtly Christian nature, their immediate reaction is 'We're not interested in that, it's boring'. Part of the problem, I've found, is not that they are uninterested in spiritual matters or indeed that they are not keen to express their thoughts and views. What usually lies at the heart of their apparent lack of interest is that matters of faith have been presented to them in a colourless and boring way.

In seeking to teach the Christian faith we should be as colourful and imaginative as we can. In this task God will help us for He is the one who is supremely creative. Through the power of the Holy Spirit He is continually doing new things within individuals and His body the Church. It is also as we seek to teach others more about the Living God that we will grow in our understanding and knowledge of Him. But it is important that our teaching should be clear. The young people need to have a real understanding of what it means to be a Christian. The greater the clarity the greater the understanding.

SOME AVAILABLE TEACHING METHODS

Guest speaker and talks

Let's start with the obvious. If you can get a good guest speaker, he or she can really bring a subject or issue alive and, if particularly gifted, can stir the group up and provide freshness and vitality. But take care: remember that the dynamics of a group change when a guest comes along – especially with young people, who can be very unresponsive with someone they do not know. It is best to invite only speakers whom you know or who come recommended for their ability to communicate with teenagers. A bad speaker can be a disaster and an embarrassment to everyone. Also, be ambitious about whom you invite. If you are sure that someone would be good, don't be afraid to ask – he or she can only say no. If your group meets after church on a Sunday night, your vicar or pastor may be pleased to have your guest to speak at the evening service, which could be an incentive for the speaker to come.

Newspaper cuttings

This can be a very effective method, particularly if you want to examine a topic – for example, famine, violence, greed, kindness, selfishness. You can get the group to go through some recent newspapers and cut out the articles that relate to the given topic. You may want to paste them up on a display board or put together your own newspaper issue. In the latter you could add the group's own editorial or letters column. Or you may wish to open up to a general discussion on the items selected. From this you will need to guide the discussion and use the opportunities to bring out any valuable spiritual or ethical points.

You may, of course, wish to produce a newspaper based on an incident in the Old or New Testament. Here you could discuss headlines and involve people in writing eye-witness accounts, adding in pictures, advertisements and interviews.

Reaction and action

Confront the group with an incident or problem. First of all, get their reaction and then ask what would be their action to solve the problem. Take, for example, an incident where someone is being bullied – what is their reaction to that and what steps would they take to cope with the situation? Other incidents or problems could deal with such issues as forgiveness when confronted by violence, or with questions of racism, of distribution of wealth, etc.

One youth group had a very successful evening by collecting together the problem pages of various magazines. In small groups they were then asked to discuss what action they would advise on the problem.

Meditation

One of the complaints about TV is that it has depreciated people's power of imagination. A good meditation may not only focus people's thoughts and feelings but also prompt their imagination. You may wish to lead a meditation on an incident in the life of Christ or a biblical figure. It takes very little just to set the scene, but each person can fill in the colour of the picture in the mind's eye, through the periods of silence. A good meditation can allow a person to enter into the event and to understand it to a greater degree.

You may wish to construct a meditation with teenagers closing their eyes and using their imagination, or you could use an object as a focus of attention – a cross or a candle.

If you allow your young people to create their own meditation to lead the group, you may be pleasantly surprised by the insights they have and the sensitivity they show.

31

Silence

Generally we tend to be afraid of silence. With friends you do not know very well, the pressure is to talk and to create activity. But the more you get to know your friends, you lose the embarrassment that silence often causes. You may, of course, find that silence in your young people's group does not work. If it doesn't, don't worry about it. But you may find, if you gradually and gently introduce silence to the group, that its members appreciate the opportunity to be still, to reflect and to listen to God.

Drama

We have got a section on drama (see chapter 25, below), but it may be helpful just to mention here that using drama can be a very effective teaching method. It can also be very enjoyable. One youth group leader who recently started up a church-based group in her village discovered that, although few of the teenagers had any Christian commitment, they loved doing sketches. All of the sketches were taken from a number of the many Christian drama books. These particular teenagers lost much of their normal reticence about religious matters as they got stuck into doing sketches on the parables or incidents which had a spiritual meaning.

Also, you may discover that some teenagers have a real ability to write short, amusing yet thought-provoking pieces of drama which they are quite happy to get their friends to enact. In fact, if I go to speak to a group which I know has some sort of interest in drama, I will occasionally ask them to write and act a sketch on the theme of the talk. It often helps the atmosphere of the evening and emphasises the message of the talk.

Added to drama, of course, are mime and dance. If you have never done either before, give it a go. You may discover some interesting latent talent.

Visual aids

We all acknowledge how important visual aids are. But often, as busy youth leaders, we are tempted to forget their importance.

A far higher percentage of information is retained when it is presented visually as well as verbally. Although we tend to think of visual aids as being a new phenomenon, it is worth remembering that Jesus was a master of using the visual. One could draw up a very long list of visual aids that He used. In fact, next time you are reading in the Gospels count the visual aids that appear. Here is just one example – a mustard seed. In fact, it is Christ who gives us the world's most powerful and effective visual aid in the bread and the wine: symbols of His body and blood given to each one of us as we take the sacrament.

A lot of visual aids are, in fact, lying all around your flat or house – items you could use to illustrate a particular point. Dare I ask how many of you have seen John 7:37 & 38 illustrated by using a jug of water and a glass? If you have not, just imagine how you illustrate what Jesus said.

> On the last day of the feast, the great day, Jesus stood up and proclaimed, 'If any one thirst, let him come to me and drink. He who believes in me, as the scripture has said, "Out of his heart shall flow rivers of living water".'

There are, of course, obvious visual aids that are available for teaching, such as overhead projectors, film strips, slides, soundstrips and videos. Buying these items can be expensive unless you are going to use them regularly. But does your local Christian bookshop hire out such items? Also, your denominational area headquarters – church or diocesan house – should have a resource centre for such items. They can usually supply you with catalogues of what is available and will often post them to you.

Games and ice-breakers

These can be very useful in establishing the right kind of atmosphere – which is important if you are thinking of teaching as a broad medium. Games and ice-breakers can help to overcome barriers of shyness and reticence. Also, they can help to break down cliques that tend to arise in any youth group, particularly if the young people go to different schools.

There is a section on games and ice-breakers (chapter 23, below), so take a look at that for some ideas.

Simulation games

These are an imaginative way of helping people understand issues and problems. What you seek to do here is to simulate within the structure of a game the pressures and difficulties that are involved with certain economic and social problems.

The best known simulation game is probably the Trading Game produced by Christian Aid. This deals with the question of Third World development. If you would like details, contact Christian Aid.

Role play

This is a very useful activity as a tool for teaching, in that it can help individuals to understand the thoughts and feelings of others. The value of role play can be particularly effective in dealing with questions of relationships. Let me give you an example. Suppose you are having an evening on the Fifth Commandment which, of course, is all to do with relationships with parents. Now, you can choose an issue or situation that causes conflict in the home as a basis for the role play. It may be the question of rules – possible conflict, say, over what time young people have to be back at home on a weekday night. You can do this any number of ways, but you may choose two teenagers – one to be the parent and the other the young person who is rebelling against the rules. Having set the issue, you ask them to talk their way through the conflict. When the exercise is over you can use it as a basis for discussion and tease out what insights they have gained from adopting the position and views of the respective parties.

You can also ask the group what situations, real or imaginary, they would like to explore, and from that probe the various reactions and consequences to what is said or done. If it is helpful, you can get people to exchange their roles and discover more of the opposite side's feelings.

Role play can also be used as a basis for teaching biblical

incidents: for example, the occasion when Jesus talked to the woman at the well in John 4. This method can be very effective in helping teenagers understand people's reactions to meeting Christ, and can assist their own understanding of what they, themselves, feel.

Discussion

You usually find with teenagers that they have no problems when it comes to talking. It is usually a problem of how to keep them quiet.

But using discussion as a medium for teaching has to be done with care. Certainly, it is often very useful and creative to break up into discussion groups and get the teenagers to talk through something that maybe you have introduced in a short talk. It can also be a real advantage to hear different ideas and opinions, and it may be that the collective opinion of the group is stronger and more informed than that of the information that could be conveyed by the teacher. However, if discussion is used too often it can actually dissipate a message that you are trying to get across to a group, particularly if it is a message which is being expressed over a long period of meeting. Too much discussion creates too many opinions and views, and the central and most important message gets lost. So take care to use discussion groups in the whole variety of ways that can be used and with the diversity of effects, and do not overdo this method to the detriment of the overall ethos of the group.

Leading a discussion group is actually a skilful art. You need to know when to let the talk flow without predetermining the outcome. You need to know when to inject certain questions and what type of questions. A good discussion leader can clarify what is being said while also enabling the discussion to move and develop at a reasonable pace. It is not an easy skill and the only way to develop it is by experience.

Interviews

It is a tradition in some churches that people give their testimony about how they became a Christian. This is an effective way of revealing how God is personally active in our lives and world today. I have also seen interviews used very successfully in youth services where an individual, or even a group of people, has got a valuable insight or experience to share. The effect you gain from a good interview is that 'this is real, immediate and relevant'. For example, you may wish to interview one or two of the young people in your group on 'How does being a Christian affect one's daily life?' In fact, within reason, the variety of aspects of the faith that you can choose to highlight is tremendous.

Also the way you use interviews can vary. You may divide and break the young people up into groups of three or four, and with a list of questions you have given them or they have drawn up, get them to interview members of the congregation you have invited along to the evening.

You can also choose a situation or incident and use it as a basis for getting the teenagers in pairs, with one interviewing the other about what happened. The effect will be that the interviewer should probe deeper into what is involved in the incident. An example of a story you could use is the arrest of Jesus. You'll probably want the interviewee to have read the story beforehand.

Just stop for a moment at this point and, taking into consideration the members of your group, think about what you want them to understand, and think of how many various ways an interview situation could be used effectively.

Face-to-face dialogue

This activity is similar to role play and interview but also different. What it requires is simply this. The members of the group, working in pairs, are asked to discuss a certain issue. The individuals are required to take different opinions. It may be best to prepare a sheet giving some basic facts. Issues that could be part of the dialogue may include the Christian attitude to war or to apartheid, or a current issue in your church.

Debate

With some youth groups debates do work well, with others they do not. There is only one way to find out – give it a try.

What you will need is a chairperson, a proposer and seconder on each side, and, of course, a subject. If the speakers are nervous and have not done this sort of thing before, you may wish to rule that speakers should not be interrupted. At the end of the formal speeches, the debate is thrown open to the floor. After all have aired their views you may have one short, summing-up speech from each side – or, indeed, you may wish to move straight to the vote.

Subjects – well!

This House believes that (THBT) Young People do not have enough say in Church affairs.

THBT Women should not be ordained priests.

The art of a good debate is to choose a good subject about which your group has some diversity of feeling. The debate will collapse if everyone agrees!!

Questionnaire

Presenting the young people with a questionnaire is a good way of finding out what they feel as a group, but it can also be useful for them to talk through what they feel about certain things.

You can organise a questionnaire based around their attitudes and values or on what they feel about Church. Their answers can be discussed that evening or collated and discussed the following week. It could even form a basis of a report to your church council.

Drawings, colours and music

Many people, and particularly teenagers, find it difficult to express their feelings verbally. Music is often able to capture and emphasise what we feel. Drawings and colours also can be expressive of our emotions. A workshop I attended at a conference at Lee Abbey in Devon was entitled 'Praying by Colours'. We were given a range of coloured paper and asked to arrange them on the floor as an expression of what we wanted to pray about. The dark colours tended to be representative of things we want to pray about – problems.

The lighter, more vivid, colours tended to express the thanksgiving we wanted to give to God. The exercise was useful and the colours acted as an enabling focus for our thoughts.

Using colours and music, individuals may be asked to express what they feel about a problem or issue or incident. The success or otherwise of this will depend on how well members of the group trust and relate to each other. The week before you do this, you may want to ask them to bring along colours or music which mean something to them in terms of mood and feeling.

Drawing can again be useful as a way of expressing an understanding and perception of something. An activity which I have frequently used is to get people to draw a map of their life so far, expressing in pictures events that have happened along the way.

Christian books

How many of you have been affected and helped by reading a Christian book? I would guess most of us. Books can be very influential. So if we constantly, but gently, encourage our young people to be reading Christian books, then that can be a positive thing. You will probably never get more than a small minority to read Christian books, but keep it on the agenda of the teaching medium of your group because certainly some will be affected by the experience.

Peter Stow, in his recent book *Youth in the City*, mentions how gripping he found *The Cross and the Switchblade* when he was a teenager. The book was relevant because it was pertinent to the kind of life he was living at the time.

To help stimulate interest, you might, every few months, want to get one of the teenagers to do a book review.

If you are not up to date on the latest and most worthwhile Christian books, go and have a word with the manager of your local Christian bookshop.

These are just some of the methods you can use in the activity of spiritual teaching. If you use any of these methods, always adapt them so that they work for your group. Also remember that what your teenagers may learn most of all is from you and the way you live your life and your attitudes and values. So let your own personal teaching be from our loving Lord and Master.

6

SOCIAL AND POLITICAL AWARENESS

He has shown you, O man, what is good; and what does the
Lord require of you but to do justice, and to love kindness,
and to walk humbly with your God?   (Micah 6:7)

Christianity is about people and Politics is about people. It is
inevitable that there should be interaction between the two.
Some Christians very much identify their faith with a particular
political cause, while others see politics and faith as being two
separate avenues of thought and practice. To adopt such
extreme perspectives can be very unsatisfactory because a
Biblical analysis of faith and a review of the history of the
Church show that faith is very much a question of social and
political awareness.

Christopher Wright, in his book *Living as the People of God*,
points out that 'God's holiness' is thoroughly practical. It
includes generosity to the poor at harvest time, justice for the
workers, integrity in judicial processes, considerate behaviour
to other people, equality before the law for immigrants, honest
trading and other 'very earthy' social matters. Also, as anyone
reading the Bible will be readily aware, one of the key
redemptive events which is of great theological significance is
the freeing of the Israelites from slavery in Egypt and their
journey to the Promised Land. This tremendously important
event, which shapes so much of the Old Testament and New
Testament, shows that God's message of redemption was not
just verbal but visible and tangible. The Children of Israel
experienced the reality of God as they were taken from injustice
and oppression to freedom and possession of a land where they
could live and enjoy the fruits of their labour. The story of

40

the Exodus is just as much a political as a spiritual story.

The essential question is, what significance does this have for a youth leader who is dealing with teenagers? The answer is that, amidst all the activity and discussions of a youth group, there should be the aim of developing young people's social and political awareness. The sad reality is that Church youth groups often possess no substantial social and political dimension; they deal only with spiritual values as they relate to individuals. The emphasis is on personal salvation and evangelism, and the general premise is that love is all you need. Such a framework of thinking will not only create naive and ill-informed young people, but it is not doing justice to the Christian message.

The mention of the word 'politics' to the majority of teenagers will usually produce a reaction of boredom and disinterest. However, as Myra Blyth pointed out in an article in *Third Way* (a Christian magazine promoting social and political awareness): 'Many young people feel very deeply about social and ethical questions. They are frightened of a nuclear war, they are scared to build up their hopes about getting a job, and they are concerned about the relationships with the police and the law.' There are many issues which young people do feel very strongly about, and the danger in not having issues raised in a Christian context is that, in fact, Christianity either becomes a subculture of thought or it is marginalised to the purely individual response.

Let's stop and consider some of the issues, social and political, which young people do express a view upon.

- Nuclear weapons
- Abortion
- Unemployment
- Racial discrimination
- Sexual inequality
- Apartheid
- Sunday trading
- Homosexuality
- Child abuse
- The Environment
- Work
- Pollution
- The Unions
- Religions and political persecution
- Poverty
- Third World development
- Education
- Pacifism

- Pornography
- Genetic engineering
- Homelessness
- Animal vivisection

If young people do have opinions on such questions, is it then appropriate that there should be an attempt to explore whether the Christian faith has anything relevant to say to these issues? The answer should be, Yes. These are issues that affect the way we live and relate to others and the world in which we exist, so it is appropriate that we should allow our young people to develop a Christian perspective in the light of Biblical teaching and the traditions of the Church.

It may not always be possible or desirable to look at all the individual issues that young people are concerned with, but it is important that such matters are related to their understanding of life and the Christian faith. For example, to look at the subject of social and racial injustice may not immediately relate to your group. However, if you begin with a statement like 'it's not fair' – a phrase often on the lips of teenagers – you can develop that and then broaden their understanding from what they perceive to be unfair to what others experience to be unfair and unjust. Issues which do raise questions of social justice in the mind of young people can be found in their experiences when they are made to feel inferior or powerless. Such feelings may be centred around an inability to perform well at games or in academic studies. It is a question of recognising where teenagers are, and of developing their spiritual awareness as it relates to themselves, their friends, their community, their country and their world.

In attempting to develop a wider social awareness with your teenagers, it is important not only to deal with issues that relate in some way to them but also to deal with specific matters. You will not achieve an increased awareness by talking about general concepts and political theories, but interest can be sparked off by raising questions of poverty, pornography and nuclear weapons as examples. However, this should not be taken as an opportunity for you as a youth leader to impose your own ideas, but rather as an exploration, in the light of

Christian teaching, of what is the possible Christian viewpoint on such matters. You may wish to express your own view so that the young people can interpret your presuppositions, or alternatively you may not wish to disclose your political standpoint so as not to prejudice the argument.

It is also important, if you are to engage young people's interest, to do something that will show the actual relevance of the issue under question. If you have a group from a suburban area and you want to look at the Christian response to unemployment or poverty, then take them to a deprived urban or rural area. In looking at Third World development, people's awareness can be greatly stimulated by having a meal where only a small minority of the group actually get enough to eat, the rest being given virtually nothing. Many of the aid organisations have simulation games which can be played to illustrate some of the aspects of the imbalance of social and political power that exists in the world. The best known is Christian Aid's Trading Game. You may also be able to use local community issues or even internal church matters as starting points for discussion. As a youth leader you may find it helpful to be on the mailing list of a number of organisations so that you know where to obtain information, ideas and material.

Inevitably, the raising of contentious matters will cause conflict. As church members we are generally afraid of conflict because we want to be seen as a warm group of people who have a lot in common and hold each other in mutual love. However, avoiding conflict can often be negative. What can be a maturing experience is learning to listen, exchange ideas and handle differing opinions. To avoid conflict inevitably leads to a superficiality of relationships, whereas to face it can draw people together provided it is dealt with in a mature way.

SOME RELEVANT ORGANISATIONS

In addition to the following, it will also be helpful to refer to the organisations listed in the Appendix of National Addresses at the end of this book.

Amnesty International [political & religious persecution]
99–119 Roseberry Avenue, London, EC1R 4RE
Tel. 071 278 6000

Board for Social Responsibility [social issues]
Church House, Dean's Yard, London SW1P 3NZ

Care Trust [social & political issues]
53 Romsey Street, London, SW1P 3RF
Tel. 071 233 0983

Christian Impact
St Peter's Church, Vere Street, London W1M 9HP
Tel. 071 629 3615

Church Action on Poverty
Central Buildings, Oldham Road, Manchester M1 1JT
Tel. 061 236 9321

Life [moral & medical issues of abortion law]
118–20 Warwick Street, Leamington Spa, Warwickshire
CV32 4QY

Shaftesbury Project [social issues]
79 Maid Marian Way, Nottingham NG1 6AE

Shelter [homelessness]
88 Old Street, London EC1V 9AX
Tel. 071 253 0202

SUGGESTIONS FOR FURTHER READING

John Gladwin, *God's People in God's World* (I.V.P.).
Fred Milson, *Political Education: A Practical Guide for Christian Youth Workers* (Paternoster Press).
Pip Wilson, *Gutter Feelings* (Marshall Pickering).
Chris Wright, *Living as the People of God* (I.V.P.).
Faith in the City (Church House Publishing).

7
HOMEGROUPS*

BASIC QUESTIONS

Why set up homegroups?

The idea of homegroups for teenagers began with my frustration at trying to teach a large group of teenagers after church on a Sunday night. When I arrived in the parish there was a group of about fifty young people who assembled straight after the evening service at about 7.45 and expected to be entertained, stimulated and filled with coffee and tuck until about 10 o'clock.

I very quickly found it a strain, at the end of a long day, to try and find ways of communicating about Christianity to such a large number in a sufficiently stimulating way to hold their attention week after week. There seemed to be problems with every method that I tried. It quickly became boring if I tried to 'lecture' from the front, and this seemed inappropriate after the group had already sat through a sermon in church only half an hour before. Nor was I satisfied that splitting into small discussion groups was really achieving understanding in any depth. Each week it was necessary to divide into a new group; there was not enough time to grow confident in each other's company, and so we never got beyond the superficial. Nor were the church facilities able to cope with trying to split into seven or more groups.

As we developed our evening services to make the worship more accessible to young people, we began to notice three

*This chapter is contributed by Geoff Willis.

45

effects. First, more and more young people came and took part in our worship. Secondly, the services became longer in duration. And thirdly, at the end of worship the teenagers began to stay in the church with the whole congregation, drinking coffee.

While welcoming these developments as moving away from having a youth group that was to all intents separate from the rest of the church and towards a group that was becoming more a part of the body, we were forced to reconsider what we were aiming to achieve in our youth group meeting.

It no longer seemed appropriate to be going straight out of church and into a heavy teaching session. Nevertheless, we still felt that there was a need to teach and give pastoral help to teenagers beyond what they got from the main services. Furthermore, we were faced with a positive situation – here were some committed Christians who did want to learn, who did want to be taught.* Meanwhile we were running a Confirmation course which involved about fifty youngsters, who at the same time were about to join in at the younger end of this youth group. This Confirmation course was done in 5 groups of ten youngsters, each group being in a leader's home. After initial awkwardness and being unsure of themselves, some of these groups really gelled – by the end of the course they didn't want to stop (even though they were already coming to the Sunday night youth meeting as well). They enjoyed meeting together; they valued having available to them the attention of the leaders; they enjoyed being able to ask questions which on Sundays, in the larger group, they were not confident enough to address.

Furthermore, looking at some of the shy members on the Confirmation course, I realised that the switch from a safe group of ten individuals to a group of fifty-plus was a nightmare. We tried to overcome this by making it compulsory

---

*This is very important, because the possibility of groups demands commitment and is therefore not likely to be suitable for non-Christian youth groups – though there are possibilities if you have a mix.

during the Confirmation course to come to the youth group meeting after church, on the basis that, if you try it only once or twice, it's terrifying; whereas if you're forced to work through it ten times, you will overcome your fear. Nevertheless, experience quickly taught me that many of the quiet ones could not stomach a group of over fifty people.

So we put these two threads together and the obvious began; we set up homegroups for them, groups which they could join at the end of the Confirmation course and which would run throughout the year.

Why homegroups, not housegroups

A fundamental part of the aim is to invite teenagers into a Christian *home* on a regular basis. Given the high incidence of family breakdown and some teenagers living away from home, we want to be able to provide a mini-alternative.

Thus, part of the aim of meeting regularly in the house or flat of someone (who is not a parent figure) is that this *home* may become in some way a bolt-hole for the teenager – somewhere and someone they can turn to in a crisis. The theory is that, if you've never been to the curate or youth leader's home before, you're unlikely to go there for the first time in an emergency. If, however, you've been there regularly on a weekly basis, when you come to cross the threshold in a crisis, you know you'll have a welcome.

How do homegroups fit into youth work structure?

In the first place, we decided not to do away with the after-service meeting on Sundays. Instead, we lightened its content in the realisation that this meeting was no longer the main teaching arena for teenagers. We now meet after Sunday service for an hour and a half, of which only half an hour contains any teaching material, the rest of the time being given over to an informal hour of chat and socialising, with free coffee and biscuits available. Obviously, the leaders are available for chat or prayer, but the main change is that we no longer spend an intensive hour on teaching.

The homegroups then, run in addition to the Sunday evenings. But I make it clear to the teenagers that, if it is a choice between the two, then I consider the homegroup to be the more important event, where the main teaching goes on, and that we hope they will make the homegroup their priority.

In addition, we meet twice a month for social events on a Friday evening.

All this obviously involves a heavy work load, something we are able to take on partly because we have a large full-time staff. It may be right in some parishes to drop the large meetings on the Sunday and meet all together only occasionally, say once a month, while concentrating on the groups.

Who are homegroups for?

Firstly, and importantly, homegroups are not for everyone.

In setting up the groups we made it clear that they were for the committed only. By 'committed' I do not mean that they are only for committed Christians, but rather that they are only for those prepared to commit themselves in principle to the group.

They need to be committed to wanting to learn more about Jesus. They need to be committed to each other – to getting to know their brothers and sisters in Christ.

For those who are not committed Christians – in the sense that they have not yet decided to follow Jesus (those whom we might call enquirers or seekers) – the group really should work on the principle of 'Come and See'. In John 1:35–9 Jesus said, in response to the disciples' first question, 'Come and See', and took them back home with Him. In going to His home they found out what He was like; they learnt to trust and eventually love Him. Our hope is that these groups in a home will achieve exactly the same thing: that teenagers might come and learn about and eventually to love Jesus.

How are homegroups organised?

The first principle that I enforced was that the teenagers do not choose which group they go into. Just as we cannot choose our brothers and sisters, so we cannot choose our fellow travellers on the Christian journey. With teenagers it is particularly important to break up cliques, and we were determined to start our groups with young people who were coming to them because they were committed to the idea, rather than simply because they wanted to be with their friends. We felt that there were enough opportunities during the week when they could meet with their friends, and that if they would only come to a group if their friends were in it, then they were not sufficiently committed to the groups. I would rather start with a small number of teenagers than get them all into groups only to find that their real motivation was purely social.

We do, in fact, practise two exceptions to our general principle of randomly allocating teenagers to groups. First: if there are some who are very shy and we feel would not be brave enough to come on their own, then we arrange for them to be in a group where they have a friend. Second: because our boys are greatly outnumbered by the girls, we ensure that no boy, unless exceptionally brave, is in a group on his own; we put the boys in pairs or preferably threes. I believe it is better to have some groups that are all girls rather than spread the boys so thinly that they stop coming. However, our principle of random allocation can easily be manipulated by the teenagers. Since the groups all meet on different nights, all they need to do is say they only have one free evening and thereby get into the group of their choice. Generally, however, we find they understand and go along with the idea that they do not choose.

Key elements in homegroup organisation are meeting times, size of group and, of course, leadership.

1 *Meeting times*. We run groups on three different nights of the week to make it as easy as possible for people to be able to attend a group. Most of the groups meet after supper, starting at about 8.00 pm and lasting about an hour and a half. Some teenagers, particularly those who come from outside the town, find it more convenient to meet straight after school

rather than going home and then coming out again. So we run a group from 5.00 till 6.30 pm.

2 *Size of group.* For an adult homegroup eight to ten people seems ideal. For a teenage housegroup around twelve seems to work better. The reason for having slightly larger groups for teenagers is that they are less regular in attendance, and we frequently find we are one or two short. Moreover, with a slightly larger number, teenagers feel more secure but are still able to take an active part.

3 *Leadership.* Leaders for these homegroups are the single most important ingredient. Prayer for God to bring in the right leadership takes up more time than any other single prayer issue.

Firstly and obviously, leaders must be committed and relatively mature Christians.

Each group should be led by a couple of leaders, one of each sex though not necessarily married. Having a pair of leaders is important. It diminishes the chance of scandal and doubles the chance of forming a good relationship with the teenager. Having one leader of each sex is invaluable, particularly because some teenage problems will relate to sex and therefore having a leader of the same sex to engage in counselling is vital.

Leaders will need to be able to teach and lead Bible study, though one leader may feel this is his or her particular strength, leaving the other to concentrate on the informal side.

Most important of all, they need to be able to relate to teenagers. In looking for a leader we are looking for a non-parent and a non-teacher figure. The homegroup is a different place, away from home and away from school (some who come straight from school change out of school uniform when they arrive to accentuate this).

Homegroups depend on leadership. You're only as good as your leaders. Therefore, to run homegroups week after week, you need very committed leaders. This can lead to many problems of stress and burn-out as people feel the strain of overburdened time commitments. A great deal of prayer and support needs to be laid on to look after those who commit themselves to this very hard work.

A problem also arises as groups grow. You will need to divide, but you can only form a new group when you have a pair to lead it. You will need to pray constantly for God to bring people in to take on this work.

AIMS OF THE HOMEGROUPS

Good and safe environment

For me (a shyish person), the idea of fifty people all gathered together is overawing. So I give up before I start. Faced with so many people I feel lost and vulnerable, and I hesitate to break into their conversations. But at home I can be me; I don't feel so vulnerable; and I have limited numbers to start to get to know. Moreover, at home the teenagers can relate to you, because they see you in your environment, eat your chocolates, break your furniture, play with your golf-putting machine. (At one early session I gave them five minutes, inviting them to go anywhere in the house, to find out as much as possible about me. they went everywhere, found out everything about what toothpaste I use – but only one really bright teenager saw the point and came to talk with me, to find out the most about me.)

You get to know a person by going home and spending time with them – that is how the disciples got to know Jesus. So a prime aim is to provide a good, safe environment to get to know your teenagers and for them to get to know you.

This is the first vital ingredient for a good group: Your planning must allow time for people just to relate to each other – the amount of time needed will grow each week as it becomes easier. This is sharing our lives, our concerns, fears, fun and just the day-to-day things that concern us all. Don't be so tied to your planned Bible study that you can't allow extra time for this kind of sharing, especially when one of the members has a lot of news and chat or has brought some photos!

In our group we always start with chocolate chip cookies,

tea and squash. It helps. Why do you think that we have so much coffee at church events? Because we find chatting difficult, we are afraid of each other, and so we need to hide behind a cup while we feel our way forward in the conversation.

Worshipping God

Teenagers have an amazing capacity to go on and on worshipping, so explore ways of worshipping in your front room.

Always pray at the start (they'll get used to it and respect it). Then sing unaccompanied or with a guitar or piano, or even a tape recorder. (Rounds are particularly effective.) Say a few short thank-yous to God (especially related to the prayers that you prayed last time, and where you have been able to see answers).

Bible-study

It is vital that you get down to Bible-study so that people can learn to enjoy the word of God. But it is important that you find ways to make it more comprehensible and really make it fun and relevant. All teenage Bible-study, I believe, should be built round the maxim 'I hear – I forget; I see – I remember; I do – I understand.'

That means that all Bible-study should be participatory. Get them to *do* things. Not only does this mean that you get them each to read round the passage a verse at a time (which also ensures that they all pay attention), but also that you should make exercises up for them to *do*. And while we're at it, let us get away from always being obsessed by words. Get them to do *things*, not only answer wordy quizzes. For example: if you are looking at the subject of 'sin', get one team to cut the bad news out of newspapers while another team cuts out the good news. Then analyse the news and what causes it. Go on to look at the bad news in their own lives – caused mainly by people, both ourselves and each other. It makes a great deal of mess but they love it.

Use books and manuals for ideas. Ice-breaker games are strongly recommended. Some are published in books. (A very useful one is Emlyn Williams' *Consequences*, published by Scripture Union.)

Read round the group a verse at a time. Act out the story. Make the Bible come alive by putting it into interviews for television. Use paper like mad; prepare graphically designed sheets to fill in with pictures, cartoons, multiple-choice layouts, etc. which they can take home. But *do* something.

And, most of all, aim to learn from them. True learning is when your teenagers find out the answers, not when they are told the answers. Ensure that you have an aim, that you know where you are going. But also make sure that your aim is achieved by their discovering things for themselves. Allow them space to relate the Bible to their own real experience. Does it really follow that I'm a new creation? Am I? Does it feel like it? Let the Bible face up to the challenge of their lives and their questions – it is well able to cope with the reality of teenage lives.

Prayer

Obviously this relates back to the initial time when people have shared what is on their minds; what they are doing and what they're worried about. It is good to allow time specifically for this kind of sharing, just before the prayers, so that people feel more confident and informed about the prayer items. How do you get over the prayer barrier? One-sentence prayers are useful here. Make it a rule that every prayer must be only one sentence, then the eloquent pray-er, who suffers from verbal diarrhoea, will not intimidate the shy. Or go round all the group and ask each member to mention one thing; write each prayer-idea on a bit of paper; shuffle the bits of paper and then get group members to pray them aloud. But make sure that there is nothing compulsory about praying out loud. Prayer can be silent, too. My group love to end with the Grace, holding hands.

Social evenings

It is good, too, within the context of a homegroup to have social evenings. Use the natural points of the year plus your particular hobbies as excuses; have a bonfire party and a Superbowl party.

Get them all to bring something they have made (not bought). Let them cook on your stove — they love getting away from their own home. And let them wash up. Get them to give and receive.

Evangelism

A good group must grow.

Obviously, there are set times in the year when new people come up from our lower-aged groups. This is particularly so at the end of the Confirmation course. We try to keep some group-continuity from the groups that have gelled on the Confirmation course, while ensuring that we mix the ages.

Some teenagers will naturally bring their friends along to the group. Thus we get a chain reaction; meet one teenager and you then get to meet his or her friends. But to be really effective in evangelism you need to be working on several fronts at once. Get the group members to see that they are God's primary tool in evangelising their friends, and that your job is merely to help. They will need a lot of motivating. Do Bible-studies on evangelism.

Appear at, or get the curate/youth leader to appear at, the school so that the faces of Christian leaders become known.

Then get your teenagers to invite their friends. There are three levels at which they can now invite their friends where they will meet Jesus:

Church service;
Large group after church service;
Homegroups.

Have evenings when you particularly encourage them to bring a friend. Social nights are particularly good for this. Once newcomers have been over the doorstep and seen that you are human and that the other members of the group are normal, then it is easier for them to come again

That moment after

Frequently, especially with the shyer members of the group, teenagers will look for an opportunity to chat one-to-one. Give them space to stay on at the end of a meeting – you'll learn so much from them as they do so. Pray with them and be prepared to take from them as well as give. Let them minister to you.

THE REAL CHALLENGE

The greatest challenge of all in this work is to be really *you* – which includes being vulnerable. Let's all drop the smooth omnicompetent leader image. All too often we keep teenagers at arm's length. We are so very conscious of our role as leader that we 'minister' to them. We are so constantly on the look-out for openings and opportunities to give them advice that we stop being real. Let's remember that the aim of the group is to get to know Jesus and to get to know each other. They come to see Christ and to see *you* – the real you. Jesus allowed Himself to be vulnerable and let people see Him being hurt. In fact, in the vulnerability of Christ we see the reality and the great love of God. So be brave, take the risk that Jesus took. Let them see you, the real you, even if that means being vulnerable. Tell them when you are fed up – feeling low – tell them when you need support. Let them pray for you, and minister to you.

You might discover that in doing so you come alive.

8
EVANGELISM

Churches everywhere must seek new ways of passing on the
faith to the children and young people growing up in the
congregation and the neighbourhood.

(Faith in the City 6:114)

The word 'evangelism' is one which has a host of connotations
for a great variety of people. Some Christians will describe
themselves as evangelical; others will use different labels. Often
evangelism is associated with street preachers and
indoctrination. But the biblical perspective is that evangelism
is to do with every Christian sharing his or her faith in both
word and action. It is to do with passing on the Good News
that God has revealed Himself in Christ.

I recently came across a lovely story which well illustrates
what evangelism really is about. The story revolves around
Brother John, a monk who lived in a remote monastery in
Northern England. He was very happy in his job, and the
special responsibilities he had in the kitchen kept him busy.
However, one day, a new abbot was appointed who proved
to be rather strict and insisted that every monk should take
his turn in preaching. Brother John was rather disturbed by
this; he did not like giving sermons since he could never think
of anything to say. But the abbot insisted that he should take
his turn.

Eventually the Sunday arrived when Brother John was due
to preach. The time came for the sermon and he ascended the
pulpit steps. He was extremely nervous and had long been in
a cold sweat. Leaning over the pulpit he said to the
congregation, 'Have you any idea what I am going to say this
morning?' The reply came back, 'No.' 'Well, neither have I'

– at which point he jumped down from the pulpit and ran into the vestry.

The abbot was furious and was hot on his heels. Giving him a good telling off, he instructed that next Sunday he was to deliver a proper sermon. Next Sunday came and again he nervously ascended into the pulpit. Looking down on the congregation, he said, 'Have you any idea what I'm going to say this morning?' Seeking to encourage him, the congregation this time said, 'Yes' – to which he replied, 'Well then, there is no need for me to tell you'; and off he shot into the vestry. The abbot, red with fury, hotly pursued him and cornered him against the cupboards. 'Next Sunday', he said, 'you will preach a full and proper sermon or there will be trouble.'

Brother John knew that there was no way he could get out of his obligation this time. So Sunday came and he ascended the pulpit for the third occasion. Leaning over, he again asked the congregation 'Have you any idea what I am going to say this morning.' This time the congregation were unsure what to say and some muttered 'Yes' and some 'No.' Then said Brother John: 'Those who know tell those who don't know.' At which point he again jumped down from the pulpit and raced into the vestry. Meekly standing in the corner, he expected all heaven to break loose when the abbot should appear. However, much to his surprise, nothing happened, and for ten minutes he stood there hearing only chatter coming from the church. Eventually the abbot did appear, but with a broad smile on his face. 'That was the best sermon I have ever heard,' he said. 'Those who know tell those who don't know – brilliant. That is what evangelism is all about.'

The best evangelism with a church youth group will be through the friendship they have with their friends at school or in the neighbourhood. In fact, if there is a group within the Church who can and will share the Good News, it will often be the young people. When young people begin to realise the power and love of Christ in their lives, they are usually keen to tell their friends about it.

TAKING STEPS

There are some simple guidelines to encourage your teenagers to share their faith.

Good teaching

If your young people are encouraged and helped to understand clearly what it means to be a Christian and live a Christian life, this will have a vital part to play. The Bible is inherently a dynamic and powerful book which expresses the wonder of what God can do for you and me – it is Good News. If your teenagers understand that this is Good News for them, then they will develop a concern to share it with others.

The Holy Spirit

Unless we allow God to use us and empower us with His Holy Spirit, we will be wasting our time. The occasions that you worship and have fellowship together must be times when you acknowledge the divine presence of God in your midst. He is already there and we are called to honour Him and be open to Him. It is the Holy Spirit which is the power of God who gives the substance to our words and worship, and without Him everything is dry and lifeless. When young people are aware of the fellowship of the Holy Spirit and His power in their lives, it can be difficult to hold them back from the job of sharing the faith.

Outward looking

If your group members just see themselves as a church club and are exclusive, then you need to shake them up and turn their consciousness inside out so that they are outward-looking. Some groups become stagnant and eventually die simply because they want to remain a closed little group and they will not invite others along. You need to give them an awareness of what is happening around them and encourage them to see beyond their group to the needs of others. How do you do that? Well, by laying on events and occasions that are not seen as just for them. You need to educate their social attitudes.

Communicating

If someone were to ask you to explain what it means to be a Christian and how you become one, do you think you could clearly articulate it? Do you think your teenagers could? Quite a number of Christian teenagers have difficulty in explaining the faith because they are not used to talking about the Gospel. The more discussion you can stimulate in the group the better, because that will help overcome the problem. It may also be helpful occasionally to do a session on explaining the Gospel to people and then to encourage the young people in pairs to explain to each other how one becomes a Christian. If you can get them to talk naturally about the faith, then they will find it easier to talk to non-believers.

Equipping the Saints

It is extraordinary how even adult churchgoers are generally ignorant on simple issues which relate to the faith and find it difficult to articulate an answer to basic questions. Listed below are the ten most common objections by young people to Christianity. Equipping your young people to be able to asnwer some of these questions to the best of their ability will help build their confidence in talking to others.

How do you know God exists?
How can you trust the Bible?
What about people who never hear the Gospel?
Why does God allow suffering and evil in the world?.
Aren't all religions the same?
Isn't faith just psychological?
How do we know Jesus rose from the dead?
Do you have to go to church to be a Christian?
Aren't all good people Christians?
What about the bad record of the Church?

When it comes to evangelism among young people, who does the job best? Simply the young people themselves! It is the teenagers who are the best evangelists and encouragers among their own age-group. They are the ones who reach their friends at school, at college and in the local neighbourhood. So equipping them to reach out to others will be your most effective form of evangelism.

EVANGELISM IS TRANSFORMATION

Mark Ashton, in his book *Christian Youth Work*, makes the very valid comment that with teenagers it is often appropriate to speak of a four-year conversion. The reason why I think this is valid is because it is very easy to obtain an emotional decision from a teenager – but evangelism is really about an inner transformation. This transformation is something that takes time to become so rooted and grounded that it affects a person's real beliefs, their values and priorities. Rallies, dynamic talks and travelling God-shows are not alone sufficient to sustain a young person in a real life-transformation. In fact, some evangelistic events are so much 'hype' that they represent the shallowness of advertisements for washing powder. It is easy for such events to claim success by testifying to the number of people who made a decision to follow Christ. But the question is – how many people are living out their decision a year or two later?

Many youth leaders will be aware of teenagers who became Christians and at first were terribly enthusiastic, but as time went on they eventually dropped out of church and the group. Also you may be aware of some young people who were very committed and involved with the church and in many ways showed the hallmarks of mature faith; yet when going off to university or college, they simply drifted away. In an age when life is a very complex experience and young people are under immense pressure from a multitude of areas, their faith in God cannot be permanent unless it is allowed to work its way through their psychological, emotional and existential development as human beings. The powerful thing about Christ's ministry is that He exposed His disciples to all the sin and suffering of life. He did not dodge the difficult issues or deliver a half-baked Gospel which spared the disciples a lot of loneliness, difficulties and, eventually, death. He showed them that what they believed in was worth living for as well as dying for. He spent three years with them before they eventually realised the full impact of what they had seen and heard. With our young people it would be naive of us to think that helping them find faith and to grow in it is not a long-term process.

EVANGELISM IS 'ON THE EDGE'

The most effective evangelism will be done with those who are on the edge of church life, for they will have some sympathy and understanding of the faith. It is extremely rare for someone to come in 'completely cold' without having some meaningful link with the body of believers. The fascinating thing is how Jesus' ministry was so often with those who were 'on the edge'. The people who were on the edge of society, such as the tax collectors, prostitutes and soldiers, were the ones who readily received the kingdom of God when they saw a genuine integrity of faith and love. Jesus also consistently discovered the presence of God in persons who were on the perimeter, and it was these people who had a real understanding of the nature of the Good News and who called forth a quality of discipleship not possible among the comfortable and the well-settled.

The implications for evangelism among teenagers is that we ourselves and our own young people should have an open-handed ministry. We should be prepared to give and share with those around us without wanting something back. Many people are hesitant in developing an interest in and commitment to the faith because all they initially see is that they are wanted for their souls and as pew-fillers. We must adopt a 'give away love' that sees each person as a human being of value in his or her own right. We must be genuinely interested in the teenagers as people, not just as potential members of the youth group or church community.

What will attract those on the edge is a group where trust

and real friendship exist, where there is a concern for social justice, where there is freedom and open-mindedness as well as direction and a clear Christian awareness. As Richard Raines once said: 'Christianity is like electricity: it cannot enter a person unless it can pass through!' So the onus is on us to give it away.

THE EVANGELISTIC EVENT

From time to time it may be appropriate to express the ongoing evangelism of our young people's group by planning a particular event. You may have the resources both financial and personal to stage it from your own church or you may wish to join together with another fellowship. Here are some suggestions about what you may do.

Guest night

You may wish to have a youth group evening which is designed simply as an occasion to invite friends along. It may possibly be a simple introductory evening with coffee and music, where you explain all the things the group get up to over the course of a year. To add to the humour of the occasion you could show slides of previous houseparties, camps and outings.

Guest service

If you are holding a youth service in church, why not use it as an occasion to print invitation cards and invite friends along? Here it is important to be sensitive because if someone comes along and realises that the prime motive for the invitation was so that they should be converted, this can, by the pressure put upon them, do more harm than good.

Some churches adopt a policy of B O P (Bring Other People) when they have a youth service taken by the young people. It's a service where they feel that they can bring their friends and the occasion will relate to them.

Concert

Staging a Gospel Concert is quite an involved event, but with very careful planning can be effective, especially when you have properly briefed the music group before you booked them.

Hitting the road

Taking your group to lead another youth group can be very effective in encouraging your members to express and articulate their faith. It can develop confidence in sharing the Gospel with others and do much to stimulate all involved. So why not take your group out from time to time?

Assemblies

It may be useful to encourage and train some of the teenagers to take assemblies in their own schools. You can simply and effectively use drama, or readings and a talk.

Coffee Bar or Non-alcoholic Cocktail Bar

Setting up something of this nature is obviously very involved but not impossible, as evidenced by the popularity of outreach coffee bars and the present use of non-alcoholic cocktail bars. Some youth groups have taken over vacant premises and run such a venture for a limited period of time. This can build very useful links with a whole range of teenagers who normally would not be attracted to any group event.

Mission

Find a good reliable speaker and you can plan a mission for a weekend or week. Such aspects to consider are: street drama, involvement with local schools, and the manner of outreach which is relevant to your situation.

It is important to remember that you cannot open every door with the same key, so in evangelism we need to recognise that many different varieties of approaches should be used.

SUGGESTIONS FOR FURTHER READING

Nick Aiken, *Creative Ideas for Youth Evangelism* (Marshall Pickering).

Penny Frank, *Children and Evangelism* (Marshall Pickering).

Michael Green, *Evangelism Now and Then* (I.V.P.).

Alistair McGrath, *Explaining Youth Faith* (I.V.P.).

Gavin Reid, *To Reach a Nation* (Hodder and Stoughton).

M. Wooderson, *Good News Down the Street* (Grove Booklets).

John Young, *The Case Against Christ* (Hodder and Stoughton).

All God's Children – Report by General Synod.

Reaching and Keeping Teenagers, research report (Monarch).

9
SMALL IS BEAUTIFUL

I think it is imperative to say that small *is* beautiful. If you are a youth leader running a small group there are many advantages in having between two and twelve teenagers turning up. The problem with a small group is more usually to do with ourselves. We allow ourselves to be intimidated by what other local groups are doing, and we tend to see them as successful because they have a lot of young people coming along. Also, leaders of large groups can be very insensitive and not realise that, by boasting about all the wonderful activities and events that they are doing with their dozens of teenagers, they can intimidate and depress those who don't have such large numbers.

If you have a small group, you are just as worthwhile and valuable as someone who runs a large group. Often the problem in the Church is that we play the 'numbers game' and that success is marked by attendance figures. Such a value system is totally sub-Christian. Although crowds do feature in the Gospels, the significant stories revolve around Jesus' encounters with individuals, Christ had only twelve disciples because presumably He felt that that was a good number to work with. Within that fellowship of twelve there were some disciples with whom Christ was closer than others. Jesus had a very special relationship with Peter and John. As Christians we are called to minister to people, not crowds. In fact, in the Gospels Jesus is often recorded as trying to get away from the crowds so that He can pray and help those individuals in real need. The crowd are portrayed as lacking in any real loyalty and understanding – which was well illustrated on the occasion of Christ's entry to Jerusalem when they cried 'Hosannah' but which soon became 'Crucify Him!' a few days later.

It needs to be said that a small group does have advantages over a large one. Some of the positive aspects are:

Closer personal relations

The relationship between members of the group and you as a leader can be of great value and extremely close. As a leader you can be a close friend and share together with the young people. In fact, you will probably find that you treat them more as adults and the friendship is more that of equals than of leader – and – teenager. The advantages of a close relationship are incalculable and will mean that the potential of the quality of your work with them will be substantial.

By contrast, one of the frustrations of a very large group is that a leader's relationship with the young people can be rather superficial. Having in the past run a youth group that sometimes had over a hundred young people attending it, I'm aware that you neither have the time nor the opportunity to get really close to all but a handful of the young people.

Nurture

Since our primary aim in working with young people is to encourage them in their Christian discipleship, the ability to nurture this is obviously dependent on the quality of our relationship with them. You may think that to give a talk on Christian relationships is encouraging members of the group to work out their behaviour pattern, but its impact will be limited in comparison with the effect of seeing how you relate to your wife, family and friends. If you have a close relationship with them they will be able to learn far more from you by actually seeing and understanding your own behaviour. The interesting thing is that quite a large number of clergy have been influenced in following their vocation by their minister or vicar when they were teenagers. The common thread to the experience is that they had a close relationship with their local pastor. They knew him well and shared a lot of experiences together. The impact you as a youth leader are able to make in terms of nurturing young people in the faith may in the long term be greater, the smaller the group you have to deal with.

Manageability

If you plan to take the group anywhere, it is far easier to handle a small group rather than a large one. In fact, a large group can be a nightmare – as any leader who has taken fifty or a hundred teenagers to a big event can tell you. The difficulties of making sure that everyone keeps together and is back at the bus or coach on time, can make even the most placid leader a little tense. There will often be someone who is late or has got lost. In fact, taking a group into London, Glasgow or any other big city is always potentially hazardous.

In a smaller group the young people are easier to control, more manageable in a crowd, and it is easier to handle the situation if someone is ill or something goes wrong. Also it is easier to handle a small group in the pleasant surroundings of your home as opposed to the church hall, where there may be an alternative crowd hanging around outside. Discipline can be a problem with a large number of teenagers, but is less likely to be an issue with a small number with whom you have a close relationship.

Availability

You will obviously have more time to spend with a small group, simply because the demands of each individual will not collectively be as great. Young people are more likely to drop round to your house for a chat when you have a close relationship with them and they know that you may have the time to spend with them. In fact, if they do call round to your house, this in itself is a very great affirmation that your role with them is being effective and helpful.

If you do run a small group, you should make your primary goal the development of good relationships in the group. Increasing your numbers should probably come somewhere further down the list of priorities. Also one must allow for the possibility that, for various reasons, a particular group may never grown in size. For example, if you are part of a small or mainly elderly community, the growth-potential of the group will never be large. Large church youth groups tend to be in suburban areas where there is high-density population. Also, if your church does not have a tradition of working with children and teenagers, it is unlikely that all of a sudden you will have a big group. In fact, the youth groups round the country which are large in numbers tend to be in churches which have a very developed youth and children's programme, and a long history of youth work. In terms of age you generally find that a large youth group is supported by a younger age range which join the group from below.

Small is beautiful; there are many good and positive aspects to a small group and as long as you view your role in a positive way and are not intimidated by others, then a lot of good will be achieved.

SUGGESTIONS FOR FURTHER READING

Nick Aiken and Patrick Angier, *Big Ideas for Small Youth Groups* (Marshall Pickering).

W. Rice, *Great Ideas for Small Youth Groups* (Zondervan).

Good Things Come in Small Groups (Scripture Union).

PART TWO

Pastoral Care

10
ADOLESCENCE

The word 'adolescence' derives from the Latin *adolescere*, which means 'to grow up'. The dictionary defines it as the period between childhood and maturity.

There is a diversity of opinion as to what age range adolescence covers. Some experts are of the belief that it is twelve to eighteen years, while others speak of eleven through to the very early twenties. There are also those theorists who reject the notion of adolescence as a distinct stage of development. But as Professor Martin Herbert, in his book *Living with Teenagers*, says: 'Adolescence is a distinctive phase of development because of dramatic changes in growth, and new developments in the teenager's intellectual capacities and sexuality.'

Adolescence has been described in a wide variety of ways, and it sometimes seems that each expert has his own particular phrase to describe it. But, however we speak of it, adolescence is *not* to be confused with the physical development of puberty. Adolescence is a question of psychological development and puberty of biological growth. Of course, the two are related but they each have their distinctive elements.

Adolescence is a period of dramatic transition, and any change involves a certain amount of stress. It is a time also which involves new experiences, new questions and the desire to take risks. On the one hand, teenagers will want to experiment and throw off some of the restrictions of the past; but on the other, they still want to hold on to the security of home and parents.

EMOTIONAL DEVELOPMENT

Dr James Dobson, in his book *Preparing for Adolescence*, has described the emotional state of this period as being that of a 'human yo-yo'. You probably are very aware from your own experience of working with teenagers that they can be so emotionally up and down. Depression is a common feature of this period and, because of all the turmoil of inner pressures, they can be explosive in their temperament, particularly at home.

Emotionally, there is the change from the tendency to relate virtually solely to members of their own sex to that of normal social interaction with members of the opposite sex.

The very young adolescents will socialise predominantly with members of their own gender. The common interest may be a sport or the same form at school. Great importance can be attached to belonging to the group. Loyalty is considered of great importance and any form of betrayal is usually acted upon by instant excommunication. As time passes, the emotional state moves away to that of attention to members of the opposite sex. Girls generally develop before boys in this area. The emotional desires and needs become that of intimacy and sharing. Somehow life seems incomplete without having a girlfriend or boyfriend. Then, of course, they begin to have an idea of what they would like to see in someone with whom they could have a long-term steady relationship.

THE REBELLION STAGE

There is an awful lot of talk about teenage rebellion. In fact, if you talk to most parents they will usually say, when there is a difficulty at home, something to the effect of 'Well, they are going through the rebellion stage!' But many experts question whether the notion of alienation, the generation gap and the rebellion stage is not more apparent than real.

The vast majority of adolescents see themselves as basically friendly people and they have a desire to relate to adults. This very positive attitude in many ways stands in contradiction to the common image that is often portrayed as being characteristic of the teenager. It is true that, within this age of social change and rapid communication, young adolescents do tend to acquire some of their values and social attitudes from outside the family and are influenced by their peers. However, as Professor Herbert points out, research has shown that basically most teenagers feel attached to their families and homes in a positive way. The majority, when it comes to matters of more fundamental concern – such as morality, and social and political issues – tend to share their parents' attitudes. A minority, of course, adopt a more idealistic view and have very different perspectives concerning social and political change. The idealism may be inspired by a philosophical or theological way of thinking, expressing a desire to aspire to a higher life-style which has a stronger integrity. The idealism also may be a reaction against the failure of society to manage itself in a more peaceable and fairer method of government.

Since, on the major issues of concern, parent and adolescent on the whole tend to agree, where does the conflict most often lie? It tends to be found with the minor issues, such as fashion, hair-style, social habits and parental restrictions. Since the teenager is in a process of change and transition, and is also being influenced by outside current trends, the minor issues will be items that need to be permanently on the agenda for discussion and debate. How often is it the case that a major row develops in families over styles of haircut, types of ear-rings and colour of hair? This is more of an example of the minor issues being inadequately handled in the family rather than of fundamental rebellion against all the familiar, accepted moral and personal values. Pressure to conform to the practices, behaviour and outward appearance of those of one's own age increases up to the age of fifteen, and thereafter gradually declines to the point where the individual creates an image of himself or herself which they feel happy with and is socially acceptable.

Lying at the heart of most so-called 'adolescent rebellion'

are simply the problems involved in the movement away from dependence on the home to a more individual, mature independence. The young people are moving from the situation where decisions are made for them to one where they are responsible and entitled to make up their own minds. What had been previously 'adopted' attitudes and values need to be personally appropriated. This, therefore, involves enquiry and experimentation, which at times can cause conflict in the adolescent – and – parent relationship.

ADOLESCENT WORRIES AND CONCERNS

Leslie Francis, in his book *Teenagers and the Church*, has done some very valuable research on the concerns of Christian teenagers in the 1980s. His work covers young people from a wide variety of denominations and is a useful insight into the attitudes Christian teenagers have towards the Church, styles of worship, sexual and personal morality, politics and society, as well as work and leisure.

It is important to summarise what are considered to be the main adolescent worries and concerns.

Self-doubt

Who am I? What is the meaning of life? What purpose do I have in living? Adolescents are capable of asking and searching into deep existential questions about who they are. It is a time of acquiring and developing, not just a superficial identity, but an identity of deeper significance and value. Piaget points out that conceptual thought is possible from early adolescence. This involves reasoning and grasping ideals.

All this can represent at times a very familiar process, and doubts about oneself and one's own value and worth are common in teenagers.

Relationships

Relationships, of course, have a significant value throughout life. For adolescents, the way they relate to others is obviously in some sense different from how they will relate to others when they come to adulthood. As we have said, the peer-group pressure exerts most influence at the age of fifteen. The teenager is under pressure to be popular, and not to be outside the accepted peer group. The pressure to conform is very great, and equally the penalties for not doing so can be very high. How you are relating to members of your own sex, how you are being influenced and also influencing others – these are indeed demanding matters at this age. There can be a lot of power-struggling in the adolescent years.

Coping with life

Pressures can be very acutely felt; and, sadly, as an expression of this, the level of teenage suicide is on the increase. Part of this is due to the need to make decisions about things which previous generations were able to leave to later in life. Linked with the pressure involved with decision-making is also that of coping with responsibility (see the section on Early and Late Developers in the next chapter).

Parents

Parents obviously figure very much in the concerns of young people. They are continually in the process of sorting out their relationship at home with them. Some parents live their lives through their teenagers. They want their offspring to do and achieve the things that they either did not have the opportunity for or were not capable of. The pressures involved in parental expectations can be considerable. The situation may become acute, particularly if a brother or sister is more successful academically or in terms of sport, music and social skills. I have seen cases where some adolescents have developed phobias or physical ailments as a reaction to the pressures put on them by parental expectations.

Another major worry concerns the issue of the stability of the relationship between parents. Many teenagers are worried about the possibility of their parents' marriage breaking up. Any argument between mother and father can be interpreted apprehensively as a sign that divorce is on the horizon. Sometimes these fears are justified, but often it is just because the teenager is unable to understand fully the nature of the relationship between his parents. Of course, if the adolescent is from a one-parent family, then the pressures can often be added to (see chapter 15, below).

School anxieties

Since school plays a very large part in the life of a young person, it features high on the list of worries. Those youth leaders who had an unhappy secondary-school education will be able to understand in a more personal way some of the worries connected with school. Few teenagers find the work easy. Some are not academically gifted. Others do not know what they are aiming for. Pressure is exerted, either externally or internally, to make decisions about subjects to study, qualifications to gain and careers to aim for, at a time when the young person may not really be sure what he or she wants to do. There may be serious problems in relationships with the staff and other pupils, and over conforming to rules. Worries which may seem trivial to the onlooker can be of great proportions to the young person. A hospital in Surrey recently admitted six teenagers who had attempted suicide in the first week of exams.

Concern about the future

As already mentioned, this can take a personal perspective, involving such matters as career and job. What am I going to do with my life. What do I hope to achieve and gain? Behind teenagers' concern for their own personal future can lurk fears about security, the value of what is done and what it all means.

Concern for the future can also be linked with the ideological and political questions of nuclear war. Will the human race survive? Such issues can be felt very strongly and be areas of major concern.

In concluding this chapter you may have the impression that adolescence is a period of immense difficulties, guaranteed to reduce any young person to a nervous wreck. As witnessed by the majority of adults, this is not the case. For many the teenage years can be the happiest time of their life. But the purpose of this chapter is simply to highlight some of the issues and pressures that can be felt during the transition between childhood and maturity.

SUGGESTIONS FOR FURTHER READING

Dr Roger Hurding, *Understanding Adolescence* (Hodder and Stoughton).
John Coleman, *The Nature of Adolescence* (Methuen).
John Conger, *Adolescence* (Harper and Row).
James Dobson, *Preparing for Adolescence* (Kingsway Publications).

11
PUBERTY

The time of rapid physical growth and sexual development in adolescence is called puberty. We and our young people need to understand the facts as well as the feelings.

Some teenagers move into puberty very early, others later. If you look at a youth group of thirteen- to fourteen-year-olds, you will see a wide range of stages of development – particularly, of course, as between the girls and the boys. The hormones control the growth and development of the body. At times development will be reasonably smooth, at other times rapid. In fact, what you have is a five-year period where there are changes in height, weight, sexual capability and physical co-ordination.

Age	8	9	10	11	12	13	14	15	16	17	18

Boys

```
Testicles develop            ----------x----------
First pubic hair grows       ---------------x----------------
Penis begins to grow         --------x---------------
First ejaculation            ----------x-----------------
Rapid height growth begins   ------------------x-------------------
```

Girls

```
Breasts begin to swell       ---------------x----------------
Rapid height growth begins   ------------x----------------
Pubic hair begins to grow    ---------------x---------------------
First period                 ------------------x----------------------
Breasts growth completed     ------------x------------
```

x – marks the average time

The chart shows the physical development of young people. Because of the complex nature of what is happening, this development does involve many pressures. The timing of these events varies between individuals, and this can cause problems since teenagers like to be the same as their peers.

As can be seen from the chart, the order of the events experienced during puberty differs as between girls and boys. Girls begin and end the sequence of events before boys. Each event can begin and end anywhere along the line, and *x* marks the average age of onset. The completion can occur up to five years later at any point between the ages of thirteen and eighteen.

Early and late developers

Those teenagers who develop early look grown-up for their age and, as a result, they tend to be treated as more responsible by adults. Added to this, they may be good at sport and, combining other factors, they may be very self-confident and popular with their own peer group. This type of individual is more likely to be the team captain or school prefect, or to exercise some other responsible position. This, of course, has its own pressures. Since early developers tend to be given more responsibility, they have to handle and cope with that. This is not easy, because if there is not a corresponding emotional development even a small task can take on the pressure of something of great significance. It requires great sensitivity to become aware of what responsibilities will be helpful to teenagers and encourage their growth, and what may 'throw them' and spoil their confidence.

Late developers look immature for their age. In a peer group they can find life very difficult because they are more likely to be teased or bullied. Also they can be disadvantaged by adults who do not take them seriously. Boys who develop late can be under considerable pressure because they have been overtaken by all the girls and most of their male peers. This may produce a lack of self-confidence and feelings of insecurity and abnormality.

Understanding the changes

All these physical and emotional changes have to be understood and can constitute a very frightening experience for any adolescent. An extreme example was the incident which prompted the start of the Samaritans. The Rev. Chad Varah began this movement after the suicide of a young girl. She had taken her own life because she thought she had a disease; but, in fact, she was simply beginning menstruation. Sadly, she had not received the information she needed to cope with her own physical change.

The leader of a church youth group needs to be aware of the processes of physical development because it will obviously be in the background of his or her dealing with teenagers. While sex education may be received at school, or on rare occasions at home, the issue will come up in one way or another in casual conversation or formally in a group.

Leslie Francis, in his book *Teenagers and the Church*, highlights some of the concerns of young people today. One of these, as we have mentioned, is self-doubt. This relates obviously to a number of issues, but part of it will be over the question of physical appearance. Teenagers are particularly sensitive in this area of their development; it is estimated that over three-quarters of them feel unhappy about their looks. They may feel too fat or too thin, too tall or too short, and added to all this they have too many spots. This lack of confidence in their physical appearance can add to feelings of self-doubt and diminish their self-esteem and sense of their own worth. As you are aware, teenagers may be very sensitive about their dress and a careless remark or joke about what they are wearing can really bruise their self-image.

Masturbation

People of all ages masturbate. How often varies from person to person. Masturbation is a normal part of physical development. However, the attitude and teaching on such matters varies within the Church. Some denominations treat it as a sin, arguing that it is a form of self-indulgence and, therefore, selfish. The Bible gives us no teaching on the matter, although some Christians make a case out of an obscure verse in the Old Testament which refers to a man's seed falling on the ground.

Whatever your views, the fact is that the vast majority of adolescent boys and very nearly half of girls do regularly masturbate. They do so for a variety of reasons, partly to do with a comforting effect, to relax or to get to sleep. Part of the reason also is the process of teenagers getting to know and accepting their own bodies. Acknowledging that masturbation is acceptable and something that is normal is helpful in building up a positive view of sex and its place within marriage. However, what is destructive is when sexual pleasure is mixed with guilt, and this can be an anxiety-provoking combination. In this area, as in so many others, young people need the guidance of caring and sensitive Christian leaders. Many teenagers can be oppressed by a tremendous sense of guilt because of masturbation. Some feel that they would like to give it up but are unable to do so. Others see it as being in contradiction to their commitment to doing what God wants. Many teenagers can be relieved of a great sense of guilt if the opportunity is provided to talk openly but sensitively about such matters. However, before such an issue is raised it is crucial that it be discussed with your priest or pastor and with your group of leaders and helpers, if you have any.

12
SPIRITUAL GROWTH

When I was a child, I spoke like a child, I thought like a child,
I reasoned like a child; when I became a man, I gave up childish
ways.   (1 Corinthians 13:11)

To talk of spirituality and spiritual growth is at this present
moment in time very much in vogue. Within some parts of the
Christian Church, however, it has never been out of fashion.
But it is interesting that even the secular youth service is now,
in its curriculum development, dealing with the issue of teenage
spiritual growth. What is meant by the term is, of course, open
to various interpretations. Some would say that spiritual and
religious development are two separate things. The majority
of Christians would, however, find it impossible to divorce
spiritual awareness from their own religious life.

Most Christians would also see individual spiritual growth
as being totally synonymous with the life of discipleship. In
a sense I think they are right. As I said in the first chapter (on
Aims of Youth Work), what we are seeking primarily to do
is to help young people become disciples of Jesus Christ. But
the point is that during the teenage years there is an inherent
spiritual development within each individual. We are by nature
spiritual beings. There is a restlessness, an enquiring spirit, a
strength of hope and a deep longing for something or someone
to satisfy our whole being. St Augustine expressed it as a void
that only God can fill: 'Thou hast made us for Thyself, and
the heart of man is restless until it finds its rest in Thee.'

For many young people the teenage years are a growth in
spiritual awareness. If a young person has been brought up
within the Church, the recognition of the meaning and value of
religious stories and Christian practice will develop. A child tends

to see prayer as merely an activity for making requests and demands of God. A young person, however, should be beginning to recognise that prayer is about a sense of gratitude and an experience of worship that has a value and worth in its own right.

Children accept without question the religious stories contained in the Bible and handed down through the Church. Teenagers, however, will begin the process of looking beyond the stories. They may reinterpret them, question their validity or even reject them because they find it difficult to deal with the historical or literary uncertainty connected with them. The change of perception and the difficulty it can cause is well illustrated by those who wrestle to hold on to faith in the face of perceived scientific evidence or indeed the questions raised by critical radical theology. Some teenagers do not necessarily confront the change from this path. Their path may be more of seeing the problems of life, and they are unable to bring together the meaning behind the Christian statements of belief and the suffering of life as it is experienced. These crises of faith that are not uncommon in the teenage years should in fact be opportunities for spiritual growth. For there is no development of belief without questioning and doubt. We should be equipping our young people to handle the conflict and the questions by offering a faith that allows movement of belief and a sensitivity to individual perceptions.

A personal movement

It is just as the teenager is going through a period of physical and psychological change that there will also be this movement of spiritual awareness. From within the Church there is often an inability to cope with this. A lot of young people reject what has been taught to them because they find it childish and juvenile. What has been presented to them may be a neatly packaged religious faith. The young may become the victims of 'processed Christianity'. They are taught to believe certain things and to practise certain activities without being given the equipment or opportunity to explore the meaning behind the words and the reason beyond the action. Too many Christian teenagers are able to arrange together the right sequence of words to express the answer that is required without actually having a reasonable understanding of what it actually means. What will follow is either a disillusionment with their faith or a superficiality of belief which will be blown away when other more meaningful activities are available.

Kierkegaard, the Christian existentialist philosopher, said: 'There is no true knowledge without experience and a personal appropriation of that experience.' God is to be known through His Son Jesus Christ. But where we often fail with young people is that this knowledge remains a dry cerebral reception of certain facts and doctrines. There needs to be an experience of God and life, and following from that a personal understanding which involves the significance and meaning of the experience. Most adolescents will see beyond the cut-and-dried answers that are often served up to them and, unless they are allowed to see more, will reject what is on offer. Ultimately, we have a God who is beyond words and is not bound by them. It is interesting that Mark Ashton refers to John White's book *Flirting with the World*, where he says:

> Jesus wept? Jesus weeps. He weeps over sheep fed on lollipops . . . He weeps over poor, deceived young people who are falsely taught by enthusiastic preachers that an instant, subjective experience at a special conference will solve all their problems and give them a zippy, automatic, Christian joy for the rest of their lives. Garbage! Lying and devilish garbage – that leads young Christians to despair, to frustration, and to the terrible sense that, if things go wrong, God has abandoned them or they have failed.

With teenagers there is often the danger that, in an effort to attract their allegiance to Christ, we actually seduce them with an attractive Christianity which is devoid of the unpleasantness and suffering as seen by the man nailed to a cross. What is needed is not just an awareness of what is offered by trusting God, the sense of forgiveness, belonging and security, but also the loneliness, rejection and suffering that goes with it.

The spirituality of a young person should also allow for the ability and opportunity to reflect. Reflection is part of the process of making personal, and appropriating, the truths and the experience. Remarks like 'Let's just pray about this' when confronted by a difficulty, can at times be a way of glossing over the problem, keeping it at arm's length and naively giving the impression that prayer solves everything.

The spiritual history of adolescents will often vary due to their church and parental background. But it is important for a youth leader to be aware of the stage at which a young person has arrived in his or her spiritual journey. In fact, the Bible often uses the notion of a journey to describe spiritual awareness and development – as in the cases of Abraham and of the Children of Israel. And, of course, as you look at the ministry of Christ, you find Him asking the disciples to follow Him. They were always on the move. He took his followers around with Him, letting them see and experience all that life had to offer. He allowed them to be confronted with life in the raw, with its sadness, suffering, disease, prejudices and poverty. Within that journey Jesus demonstrated the involvement of God the Father and the Spirit in each situation. He allowed the disciples to see the breaking in of the Kingdom of God. From that they were able to grow and understand the meaning of life and the value of those around them. Also Jesus, in journeying with the disciples to Jerusalem, spoke of his approaching death. In doing so He sought to help them understand that the true meaning of life is of loving self-sacrifice – 'If anyone would come after me, he must take up his cross and follow me.' This means you have got to look beyond the words that are offered to you and perceive more clearly the attitudes and feelings that the person is expressing. An understanding of this is not gained overnight, but rather over weeks and months. The type of questions which can open up your understanding of where teenagers are in their journey, are:

What are their insights?
What has caused them great joy?

What has produced great emotional pain?
Who do they most admire?
What is of greatest value to them?
In what ways do they meaningfully express their faith?

A total awareness of what you are looking for is probably expressed by their development of:

Wonder: responding to beauty, order and complexity in the world and being aware of the mystery inherent in God, life and creation;

Reverence: having respect for a spiritual view of life and for ultimate values;

Compassion: expressing and valuing love, concern and forgiveness;

Curiosity: raising questions about life and about faith;

Self Respect: valuing themselves as unique human beings and recognising their contribution to others;

Integrity: valuing truth, being honest about their feelings and attitudes, and having regard for the views of others;

Commitment: treating seriously the search for meaning and direction in life and the formation of their own allegiances and commitments..

Spiritual freedom

Karl Rahner, the eminent theologian, pointed out that the key to being truly human is freedom. He added that moral action becomes more authentically human the more it is based on freedom. The spiritual growth of an individual young person will be very much bound up with the freedom to say Yes and No. 'Yes' to the truths of the Gospel and 'No' to that which denies the individual's value as a unique human being. Saying No to premarital or casual sex, saying No to pot or hard drugs, saying No to consumer values – this is just as valid a spiritual development as deciding to spend ten minutes every day in prayer. This realisation is a challenge to all those Christians working with young people. Unless young people have interpreted, understood and then made the free choice of deciding on a spiritual path and direction, their God-given humanity will not grow and develop.

Let me illustrate this. Some years ago I went on a ski-ing trip with a Christian organisation. Each evening we met together for worship and a talk. The young man giving the week's addresses was in his early twenties. He was a very lively, energetic and pleasant individual. His talks were theologically sound, imaginatively presented and delivered with great flair. But they were hollow. As the week went on this hollowness became more evident. This young man had been brought up in a very committed Christian home. He had regularly attended church as well as Bible-studies and prayer meetings. He had a real enthusiasm for God. But it was all hollow. His words and actions had no depth because he was merely echoing the words and actions of what he had been taught. He was not aware of this and I could see that spiritually he was in danger of 'falling away' unless there was a real, mature development. There needed to be an exercising of his own personal freedom at a far deeper level if he was to stand on firm ground and truly understand all that had been taught him. Possibly because of the sheltered background he had come from, there was a lack of experience in faith and living. There had been little reflection and virtually no substantial personal appropriation of the spiritual truths he had received.

If young people are to develop their spiritual and moral life within the environment of your youth group and the church, there needs to be a balance. This balance is between giving them the instruction and teaching that is needed, and allowing them, on the other hand, the freedom to challenge, question, doubt, evaluate and, at times, reject the personal implications of what is being taught.

Finally, it is worth remembering that growing closer to the love of God never ends. So all of us, both young and old, will need continually to reflect and interpret the real meaning of God's love in each situation and circumstance.

The Eternal

An inherent part of the spiritual development of any person is the sense of *The Eternal*. Some denominations within the Church have fostered this side of our awareness very well and have encouraged the mystery, awesomeness and wonder of God. Others have made it a very stark, cold and processed faith that is to be simply understood and obeyed.

As we have already said, we have a God who is ultimately beyond words. Also He is beyond our thoughts, imagination and ability to understand fully. He is, of course, known yet unknown. This is the mystery of faith. The psalmist expressed this: 'Great is the Lord, and greatly to be praised, and his greatness is unsearchable' (145:3). If we rob the faith of this deep sense of the eternal, we will be doing a great disservice to a person's spiritual development.

To return again to the Psalms, we are advised: 'Be still, and know that I am God' (46:10a). Fostering a sense of stillness among young people is a real struggle. The pressure on them is to be up, about and doing things all the time. But there must be an opportunity to be still and to listen, wonder and reflect. If you can encourage silence in your group, and with it a sense of relaxation with one another, then it can be very powerful. In the silence you may wish to use symbols to concentrate the meditation – a candle, a cross, a crucifix, a flower or a picture. Or indeed anything that encourages them to look beyond the immediate to something deeper.

In an age when people are judged for what they do, the Christian needs to focus on the fact that we are each of equal value, because of what we are as people and children of God. Part of realising who we are, and who God is, is the ability to stop and be silent.

St Paul reminds us very strongly of where our vision should be: '. . . because we look not to the things that are seen but to the things that are unseen; for the things that are seen are transient, but the things that are unseen are eternal' (2 Corinthians 4:18). As Christians we are called to focus on the unseen. We do this through our prayers, meditation, worship, reading and service. We, therefore, must be careful not to reduce all these activities to neatly packaged events and experiences so that any sense of the mystery of God and faith is excluded.

I became very aware of this side of our spiritual heritage when I went with a group of young people to Taizé. Taizé is an ecumenical community in France which attracts tens of thousands of young people every year who come and take part in its life and worship. The style of worship is extremely simple – prayers, silence and singing. The sense of mystery is captured, not only in this, but also in the icons and candles around the dimly lit chapel. The number of young people who have found God at Taizé is incalculable. But what the worship really expresses is the unspeakable mystery of the Greatness of God and His love for the world.

Corporate development

When St Augustine remarked, 'He cannot have God for his father who refuses to have the Church for his mother,' he was capturing a truth that realises that no one is an island. We cannot talk of spiritual growth as a purely personal development that has no reference to the company of believers. If we are to grow spiritually, an understanding that we are part of a much wider body is essential. Indeed, we are part of the 'body of Christ' here on earth which is sustained by the sacraments, by its worship, by its service and through the power of the Holy Spirit.

There is no question of a purely individual path of faith. Anyone working with teenagers needs gently to develop their awareness of the corporate allegiance to the 'body of Christ'. A test of spiritual growth and maturity is the degree of personal commitment to the Church and its on-going life.

13

COMMUNICATION SKILLS

COMMUNICATING WITH YOUNG PEOPLE

The most important thing to remember from this chapter is this: at the heart of good relationships is good communications. This is at the very core of what we, as Christian youth leaders, are seeking to do. You may have the most exciting and dynamic programme, but it will be practically worthless unless you are communicating and relating to the young people. It is good relationships which make life worthwhile and satisfying. The time you spend simply talking and socialising with your teenagers is just as valuable as the Bible-study or talk. Good communicating involves listening and being listened to. It involves sharing difficulties and problems as well as having a joke and a good time.

Many people feel rather intimidated by teenagers and lack confidence in communicating with them. But communication, like any other gift, improves with practice. Soon you overcome your shyness and learn how to relax and have a good 'natter' with almost any fourteen- or seventeen-year-old.

But before we move on, I would like you to take a trip down memory lane. I would like you to recall the days when you were a teenager, particularly when you were at the age of the group of young people you are now dealing with. You may want to take a pen and a piece of paper and just jot down a few thoughts. I would like you to ask yourself a particular question: 'When I was a teenager, which of the adults could I most readily relate to?' Was it those who

- took you seriously?
- listened to you?
- helped you practically?
- sympathised with you?
- could accept you as you were?
- supported you in what you wanted to do?
- offered you a challenge?

One of or all of these activities may remind you of a person or a number of persons who fulfilled the part of adult people you could relate to. Are there any other activities you would like to add to the list from your own teenage experience? Turning the clock back to your adolescent years can be helpful. Can you remember how it felt? What made you happy or angry? What were your emotional needs at the time?

I find thinking my way back to when I was fourteen helpful in relating to my teenage sister. I continually underestimate her strength of feeling and maturity of thought. But it's when I remember what I felt at her age that I begin to treat her more as a person of importance and with valuable emotions.

LISTENING SKILLS

Teenagers can often feel frustrated because they are in the difficult process of developing their ability to communicate. There will be times when this frustration will explode into remarks like, 'No one cares, no one understands me'. Often a remark like, 'I'm bored', is a gloss on what is a deeper feeling of frustration which is not easily expressible in words that pinpoint what young people actually feel.

That is why listening skills are so important. This kind of skill involves allowing enough time to talk through problems, and providing opportunities where our teenagers can explore their feelings without feeling they are being judged or criticised.

The true skill of all good listeners is that they not only hear the words that are spoken but are also sensitive to the emotions behind the words. They can empathise with someone by simply understanding the situation from the other person's viewpoint. Stop and think for a moment of those of your friends whom you would consider to be good listeners. What is it that you appreciate about them when you are talking to them? Is it that they make you feel they have got time for you? Do they give you their complete attention? Is it that they don't interrupt, or that they really express an interest in whatever you are saying?

Another important part of listening skills is your body language. I was recently talking to a clergyman who, while I was in conversation with him, began gradually to move away from me. In this extreme example, body language spoke louder than words. I realised he did not want to talk to me!

Here are some pointers as to how to use your body to emphasise the fact you are listening to someone.

Maintain eye contact

When you really are listening to someone and there is a rapport between you, you are constantly maintaining eye contact. It is not a question of staring but rather of giving the person your undivided attention. By contrast, there is nothing more frustrating than talking to someone who never looks at you. Similarly, a bad preacher is someone who never has eye contact with his congregation but rather always looks three feet above their heads. Eye contact is important.

Relax

This is so crucial but actually very difficult. In listening to someone, you may be under a certain amount of pressure because you realise that the other person has various expectations of you. If teenagers come to see you about something that worries them, you may be under the pressure of wanting to make sure they leave feeling more at peace and having received an answer. This is not always possible.

Remember, just relax. You can probably do more good simply by listening and giving your attention, so that the person can talk freely, than by giving any sort of advice.

Face the other person

This obviously is linked with eye contact. Although you can look out of the corner of your eye, by simply facing someone you are saying: 'I'm here, you have my attention!'

Keep an open posture

If your arms are open and your body is facing the person, you are sending a message. If your arms are closed and your legs crossed and your body is facing in another direction, then you are also sending a message – but that message probably is: 'I'm not interested and I'm not sure I want to listen to you.' An open posture is a sign of interest and a preparedness to be responsive to the individual.

Lean toward the other person

This is a way of saying, 'I'm interested in what you are saying'. But mind you don't smother the person! That can be very off-putting. Equally, like the clergyman I spoke of just now, if you lean away or move away you are saying that you do not want to communicate.

Take care with 'touching'

Touching is an important communication skill, but with young people it needs to be exercised with great sensitivity and care. In dealing with members of the opposite sex, it is probably best never to touch them, unless there are other people around and the gesture is relaxed and obviously understood. Sharing the 'Peace' in church in terms of a kiss or hand-shake or an embrace is a lovely way of enjoying the fellowship of God's presence with His people. The laying-on of hands is a powerful means of communication, but again it needs to be exercised with care.

Touch can reinforce the communion between one person and another, but do remember the individual and the context of the situation you are in.

*　　*　　*

Finally, we must not neglect — in our desire to achieve good one-to-one communication — that skills are required from us in the area of *general* communication.

The great power and joy of the Gospel is the wonderful news that God wants to communicate to us. This is something that is totally radical and life-giving and life-changing. It is this good news in all its richness and variety which we want effectively to communicate to the young people for whom we have a responsibility. Chapter 5, on Teaching, lists a wide variety of the ways in which we can communicate. We owe it to our Lord and to our young people to expound the faith in the most imaginative and interesting way we are able.

In terms of communication, it is interesting to note that:

Message received by	*Percentage retained after*	
	3 hours	*3 days*
a) Hearing only	70	10
b) Seeing only	70 +	20
c) Hearing and seeing	85	65

So a youth leader who wants to be an effective communicator not only on the one-to-one but also on the one-to-group level, needs to utilise the visual medium. If you have not read the chapter on Teaching, I suggest you refer to it and use the ideas suggested there.

14
PARENTS

DEVELOPING AN ALLIANCE WITH PARENTS

I'm afraid I am writing this chapter with a slight sense of guilt. For the four years during which I ran the parish youth group that I was previously involved with, I don't think that I ever gave much thought to the parents of the kids who came along. But I don't think that I was unusual. In fact, I recently came across a church youth worker of forty years' standing who admitted that in his early years, as far as he was concerned, parents might as well have not existed. We have both come to realise, however, that parental support is a crucial part of the ministry to teenagers.

As youth leaders, our links with the parents will range from the non-existent right through to close working ties. Also our experiences will be varied. Some of you may find that parents are at times among your greatest supporters, and other times they are your worst enemies.

It is very encouraging when you bump into the mother who says she so appreciates what good work the youth group does for her daughter. You feel a little embarrassed because you have never met the mother before, but you feel good because it is a positive witness for the Church. Then you also speak to the parents after morning service who express gratitude for the recent event you ran which their two children enjoyed so much. All of us get from time to time that sort of positive feed-back.

However, you may, of course, have the complete opposite. Some parents complain because what you have laid on interferes with family plans. Possibly they are unhappy that their son or daughter spends too much time at church events, and school work and other activities are being neglected. At times it may appear that the only occasion that you hear from parents is when they criticise something. Possibly they have misinterpreted a conversation with their teenagers, and this has made them feel unhappy about what went on during a particular social evening or weekend away.

Misunderstandings do arise. I was especially appalled when, through the headmistress of a local school, I learned that a parent of one of the girls in my Confirmation class was saying that her child was being brain-washed. The accusation (which I only heard of secondhand) came after a weekend away with the candidates. The young people had been challenged to make a personal acceptance of Christ as their Lord and Master. The weekend involved a lot of discussion and talk, and for those whose Christian understanding was minimal, the idea of commitment was fairly alien. The way the experience had been interpreted and then relayed to the parents only served to increase the misunderstanding. Because of the distance between myself and the parents, a false impression had developed, and this unfortunately grew out of all proportion. It took some months for us to achieve a good mutual understanding.

Some parents may feel you are being either too strict or too casual about implementing club or group rules and regulations. While some may consider that you have dealt with an issue fairly and have not in essence let the situation get out of control, others may believe that you are letting the young people get away with too much. You may, ironically, find that at times the non-church parents have a better understanding of the young people than those churchfolk who expect everyone in the youth group to be near-perfect angels all the time.

At this point, let us consider the question: What should the relationship be between the youth leader and the parents of the teenagers in the group?

Trust

Usually most parents will have an in-built trust of anything that goes on under the umbrella of the Church. (If it is connected with the Church, then it must be promoting good morals and values.) In most cases a youth leader can reckon on that degree of 'basic British' trust. It is something that is inherent in our society and is usually a good positive starting-ground.

If I was directly involved in a particular youth group, I would take an approach different from the somewhat casual manner towards parents which I had previously employed. I now believe it is crucial to build up the trust between you and the parents of the young people. That trust can overcome misunderstandings and it can also achieve a considerable number of other positive things.

If you have gained the trust of the parents, you will have often done a lot to secure the support of their teenagers. If the parents feel it is a good and valuable thing for them to attend the group, then they will do what they can to encourage their teenagers to be present. At times the teenagers will need no encouragement but this situation will not always prevail, and mother and father can be very helpful in encouraging on-going participation.

Also, if the parents can see that you have the real interests of their young at heart, they will regard you as a valuable ally in the personal and spiritual nurture of their teenagers. They will recognise that there are things that their young will talk to you about which they will not mention to them. From time to time parents would come to see me because they were concerned about some area of their relationship with their teenagers: areas in which they felt I could be helpful because of my unique role as the youth group leader.

In building up this trust it is we, as the youth leaders, who will usually have to take the initiative; for parents often exist in a separate world, particularly if they are not connected with the Christian community. But even if they care, their work and social circles may mean that, unless we make an effort to get to know them, the relationship may never develop beyond a pleasant 'hello' at the back of the church. As regards those parents you do come into contact with, make a special effort to talk to them and get to know them. With other parents you may need to take the opportunity to call on them one evening at home. One church I know has a parents' evening once a quarter to which all the parents are invited. Possibly once a quarter is rather too frequent but it is certainly something that is worth considering at least once a year. You could use the opportunity to outline the plans you have for the coming year and also to seek the parents' reaction to all that has been part of the youth programme over the previous year.

Accountability and consultation

Whether we find it easy or not as youth group leaders, we are – and indeed should be – accountable to the parents. To try and avoid this or just simply neglect it will inevitably cause disquiet and, at times, conflict. For, although an evening or event is planned specifically for the teenagers, it is not solely they who are the audience or participants. There is a shadow audience – the parents. They are inevitably involved at all sorts of levels of interest. At very least they provide the money which pays for the evening out – ice-skating or swimming or weekend course. If news gets back that safety was not observed, or decent behaviour encouraged, you are likely to have a lot of dissatisfied parents ringing you up.

However, if you recognise that in your involvement in youth activities you are accountable to parents, then you take an important step towards avoiding unnecessary conflict and towards gaining their confidence. The best way to demonstrate that accountability is simply to inform them of what you propose to do. Let them know about your programme of events and the general policy for working with their teenagers. Use the weekly notice sheets or church magazine, and from time to time write to the parents. Basically parents will support what is happening if they know what is going on. So let them know.

As well as being *accountable* to parents, we should also be in *consultation* with them. Why? Because the truth of the matter is that the parents know their teenagers far better than we do. We may like to think that we know our young people very well, but it is the parents who have known them from birth.

They are aware of their character traits, their personal idiosyncrasies and their strengths and weaknesses. Talking with parents and confidentially consulting with them can often throw a great deal of light on a young person's behaviour and attitudes. If we are truly trying to get alongside our young people and to understand them, can we do this without knowing what they are like at home, or without gaining valuable insights from those who have fed and cared for them for years?

A lady came to see me one day because she was concerned about the behaviour of one of the teenagers. The situation was that the young person's mother was very ill and this particular teenager was doing absolutely nothing to help in the difficult circumstances. The mother had come to see me to find out if I could encourage her girl to be more helpful. What was particularly sad about the situation was that the girl was one of the keen Christians in the youth group. In reality there was an inconsistency between her profession of faith at the group and her activity at home. I had not been aware of this at any point during the time I had known both her and the family, because I had not bothered to make myself aware. I had failed to encourage the girl in her pastoral and spiritual needs because at no time had I consulted with the parents.

'Consultation' with parents does not have to be a formal affair, with parents being induced to give away confidential information about their offspring. A good consultation will often be over a cup of coffee and a chat about how Sue or John is getting on.

Consultation with adults can also be valuable in regard to the mature and positive advice it may elicit. It can help avoid the consequences of hasty ideas or ill-conceived activity such as are likely to arouse the wrath of concerned parents. A midnight hike, probably greeted with great enthusiasm by the teenagers, may justifiably cause great concern in parents who can envisage some of the dangers such an activity may encounter. For any event that is planned, informing the parents beforehand and requiring a permission-note creates a sense of their being consulted. If parents feel consulted and that any comments they make are listened to, then you may gain their support and confidence.

PARENTS: A BIBLICAL PERSPECTIVE

This subject merits a separate book in its own right. The Biblical material that relates to parents and their responsibilities is considerable. It is significant that the commandment which immediately follows the first four relating to God, is about child/parent relationships: 'Honour your father and your mother as the Lord your God commanded you . . .'

St Paul in the Epistles also takes up the question of the respective responsibilities of parent and child. The opening verse of Ephesians 6 usually causes concern among most teenagers. However, the important thing that a youth leader has to recognise is that, from a Biblical viewpoint, the centre of activity of God's concern focuses around the relationship between parents and their young. It is crucial to understand this because, if such is the focus of God's attention, then it should be the focus of our own thoughts and actions.

There is no Biblical teaching on youth group leaders but there is a mountain of material on families. Recognising this should diminish the risk of our seeing ourselves as proxy parents or the youth group as another family. If the emphasis of the group seems to detract from family life rather than to build it up, then our actions are at variance with the intentions of God.

There is not the opportunity here to develop the Biblical theology of family life, but this is a very worthwhile theme for you to examine in a leadership team, or indeed as a series of study-discussions with your young people.

SUGGESTION FOR FURTHER READING

John White, *Parents in Pain* (I.V.P.).

15
DIVORCE

PASTORAL NEEDS OF TEENAGERS WITH
DIVORCED PARENTS

All of us are aware that the rate of divorce is reaching alarmingly high proportions, and it is something that the community of the Church is not immune from. You probably have teenagers in your group whose parents live apart, are divorced or have remarried. Indeed, it is sadly inevitable that in the next year or two the same fate may befall the parents of one or two of your young people.

In a recent discussion with a group of thirteen and fourteen-year-olds, the youth leaders were alarmed to find that the issue most of the young people worried about was the possibility of their parents divorcing. Leslie Francis states, in *Teenagers and the Church*, that his survey among churchgoing youth revealed 61 per cent agreeing that divorce was becoming too easy. This high percentage represents a strong anxiety about the effects of divorce.

What factors and circumstances should we specially consider, in order to heighten our awareness of the pastoral needs of teenagers who have gone through or who are experiencing the trauma of parental divorce?

Young people experience their parents' divorce as a terrible loss. The feelings can be very similar to those experienced in the bereavement process. Some teenagers have asserted, in their anger and unhappiness, that they would have found it easier for mother or father to have died rather than to have left home, particularly if that moving away involves another partner.

Teenagers often have a great sense of guilt about what has happened to their parents, amounting at times to a feeling that in some way the divorce is an outcome of what they have done, or not done. The anxiety over any difficulties or problems with which they have burdened their parents, may express itself in guilt. There can be a desolating 'if only' feeling. If only I had kept my room tidy and done more of the washing up – maybe mother would not have been so unhappy and left home. If only I had respected my father a bit more, done more of what I was told to do and brought home some decent school results, then . . . The teenagers may blame themselves for what has happened and feel, rightly or wrongly, that they were one of the contributing factors to the break-up of the family home.

On the other hand, the feeling of hurt over what has happened is not always obvious. Some young people manage to bury it. If any help is available to the family it usually goes to the parents. As long as the teenagers are manifesting no obvious signs of being unable to cope, then everyone assumes that they must be handling the situation satisfactorily. This is a wrong assumption. Considering that adolescence is a painful period, divorce can greatly intensify the feelings of insecurity, uncertainty and inadequacy so typical of the teenage years.

The most helpful thing in pastoral care for young people afflicted by parental divorce is to provide, in your relationship with them, an environment in which they can talk through their feelings. You have got to allow them to express themselves, otherwise they will bottle up their emotions and that will eventually cause them to react in unhealthy ways. It is very surprising how people are confused when teenagers start to behave in unacceptable ways when it seems that enough time had elapsed since the divorce for them to accept what has happened. It is usually a sign that no one in fact has got alongside them and helped them to work through their feelings. They must be allowed to *grow through* the trauma rather than simply *go through* it. Otherwise the bitterness may linger for many years.

Often there is a DENIAL of the situation, typified by statements like 'This can't be happening to me'. There may be ANGER, expressed in 'It's not fair!'; then BARGAINING 'possibly if I do something good or something that will attract attention, my parents will get back together'; then DEPRESSION – 'I'll never get married' or 'I'll never be happy again'. And finally ACCEPTANCE – 'I have a problem', 'I need help', 'Let's talk'. These are some of the stages that teenagers go through when confronted by the problem of how to cope with divorce.

The experience of divorce may also alter the personal growth rate of the teenager. Such a traumatic event can either slow the process down or project the young person towards an independence which is more a characteristic of people in their twenties. Some teenagers will remain closely dependent emotionally on one of the parents. They cling on to that parent out of a sense of insecurity. The fear and uncertainty can retard the natural maturing process whereby the young person gains his or her own sense of independent identity. And some, as I have said, will move away from both parents, wishing to cut their involvement with them.

One of the most difficult things young people have to deal with is their changed perception of parents. A teenager can have an idealised view of his mother and father, which at times makes them into less than real individuals. The perception of the parents can, through divorce, change from a fairly positive to very negative one. Such a change is very difficult to deal with, especially when it concerns someone so close and whom you love. While parents may have encouraged their children to face up to difficulties at school and in personal relationships, this may seem to be hollow advice when they are not prepared to do the same when their marriage is not working out. A lot of what parents may have said in the past may seem to be outright hypocrisy in the acrimony and confrontation that takes place in a marriage break-up. Confidence in the moral and personal integrity of one or other of the parents can be badly shaken. That can also alter the confidence of the young person.

Another pressure on young people created by divorce may be financial. Father leaves home, the family house may have to be sold for something more modest. Mother may have to go out to work to support herself and the family. Some teenagers may have to change schools, particularly if they have previously been to fee-paying schools.

Pressure may also come because the network of friends of their parents may change. If they remain with mother, she may spend time with other females who can give her the help and support she needs.

Jealousy may also arise if mother, in an effort to develop a new social life for herself, attempts to look younger and possibly becomes competitive with older female teenagers. The sense of jealousy can also arise if either of the parents starts seriously seeking the company of someone who is not much older than the teenagers themselves. This may particularly happen with fathers, as they will tend to date younger women.

There is clearly going to be the whole problem of conflict of loyalties. The teenager may feel more emotionally attached to one parent. A daughter may feel very close to her father but if he is the one who has left the home, then a conflict is there. She feels attached to father but he has left her and the family, and she feels obliged to support mother. The teenager will go through the dilemma of what degree of loyalty to show to each parent. This may be felt very acutely because young people will invest a meaning and message for each gesture that is made to either parent. How often should they see their mother? To what degree should they physically and emotionally respond to the parents? How do they handle questions when one parent wants to know what the other is doing and whom they are seeing?

The problem of loyalty is never more difficult than when the marriage is breaking up and becoming acrimonious. The young person can be caught between the two factions and confused as to the degree of allegiance he or she should give to either or both parents.

Pressure is also increased when the eldest teenager in a family is forced by circumstances to become the proxy parent. All of a sudden the eldest daughter is forced into a domestic mothering role because mum is no longer around. The eldest boy is forced to become the father-figure and do the jobs which had previously been done by the now absent parent. Not only do they have to handle the pressure inherent in the new role they have been forced to adopt, but they are additionally burdened by a tremendous sense of responsibility. They now feel involved with, and in a stronger way responsible for, the younger members of the family, the financial situation and the everyday details of home management.

These are some of the pressures and difficulties that a youth group leader needs to be aware of in caring for a young person who is experiencing the trauma of divorce. If you understand what they are going through and, because of your knowledge, you establish a close rapport with them, then you can be very effective in your Christian care. But a note of caution. If you happen to be married with a secure family, you may present the picture of an ideal home to the young person. They may prefer to be in your home rather than in their own and become very dependent on your situation. You need to exercise responsible sensitivity to protect yourself and your family, and to help the young person to face up to his or her own situation in a positive and mature way.

SUGGESTIONS FOR FURTHER READING

Carolyn Nystran, *Mike's Lonely Summer: A Child's Guide through Divorce* (Lion Publishing).

J. Swihart and S. Brigham, *Helping Children of Divorce* (Scripture Union).

16
BEREAVEMENT

PASTORAL CARE AND DEATH OF A PARENT

It was early one Saturday morning. I was upstairs in the bathroom when the 'phone rang. I threw on my dressing gown and raced downstairs. It was the vicar's wife. She sounded rather tense and upset. I soon found out why! Joan was dead!

Joan was one of those people who are the salt of the earth. She was a deeply committed Christian and, because of her strength of character and faith, she was an inspiration to everyone. She had been a loving wife and mother to her husband and three teenage sons. She was known and respected by hundreds of people in the community and the church. She had gone into the local hospital on Thursday for a routine operation and by Sunday it was expected she would be at home. That morning, she had died suddenly from a blood clot on the brain.

I put the 'phone down and walked into the kitchen and burst into tears. After a few minutes I managed to regain my composure. The most difficult part of the day was yet to come. George, the youngest son, was away that weekend with the youth group and knew nothing of what had happened. I decided that the only way to handle the situation was for me to travel down with one of the brothers to where the group was staying and break the news to George. After I had changed I got into the car and went round to the family home. Ted, the father, and the two boys were in a state of shock. There is not a lot you can say in such circumstances; words seem too inadequate considering the intensity of what everyone feels.

We talked for a while and Ted said that he thought it would be a good idea if I went down with John to tell George the tragic news and then bring him home.

When John and I arrived at the Centre an hour or so later, everyone was out in the adjoining field either sunbathing or playing football. They were obviously having a great time and spirits were high. However, when George spotted the two of us he began to realise all was not well. We took him into a room and gently broke the news about Mum. The three of us talked and cried and sat in silence. After a while I slipped out and gathered together the rest of the young people to tell them what had happened. They were devastated and didn't know what to say or how to express what they felt. We prayed.

After fifteen minutes a group of George's close friends came with me and we went to comfort him. After a long 'phone call to his father, he decided that he would in fact stay till the end of the weekend. It seemed the right decision for a variety of reasons, not least because of the tremendous support his friends could give him.

I wish I could say that what happened on that day was an isolated incident, but sadly it was not. Joan's death was sudden and totally unexpected, but there were many other occasions when the mum or dad of one of the teenagers died slowly of cancer or some other illness. The intensity of feelings in those situations was not quite the same but the depth of emotional pain and suffering was just as great.

As a youth leader confronted by a teenager who is experiencing the death of mother or father, you will often feel inadequate and totally helpless. At times you may even feel a sense of panic about how little you are able to do or even about how effectively you can assist the young person. Be assured that such emotional responses are common among those who are part of the caring professions and who have to deal with death and dying on a daily basis. These feelings are part of the cost involved in trying to reach out and minister to others. Such emotions are not confined to dealing with bereavement. Also, the fear of encountering such feelings should not be allowed to inhibit your care for others. At times you may recognise your need to be assured that the help you are giving to the thirteen-year-old girl or sixteen-year-old boy is of value. If you do not get that encouraging assurance, do not feel depressed. There are many, many occasions when you will question the value of your care and whether it is useful. But the truth is that often we do not know, and at times we will never fully find out. Such doubts are common.

A friend of mine who is a doctor was working on Casualty one night when a victim of a road accident was brought in. Despite strenuous attempts to save the victim's life, he died soon after entering the hospital. An hour or so later the man's wife arrived and Helen had the job of telling her the sad news. She told me that at the time she didn't know what to say, as any words of comfort seemed totally inadequate in the circumstances. All she could do was to sit down with the woman, put her arms around her and cry with her. After the incident Helen confided in me that she just felt totally inadequate and so helpless. However, sometime later she received a letter from the woman, which expressed real gratitude for what she had done that night and how she had helped and supported her. At the time Helen was not aware of the full extent of the help she was giving.

Two of the young people in my youth group had seen their mother slowly dying of cancer. The treatment she had been given had been difficult and prolonged. Eventually, after about nine months, she died. On the day of the funeral I stood outside a packed church waiting for the family and the coffin to arrive. At the time I not only felt totally inadequate but also remorseful that I had been unable to get alongside the two teenagers during the time of their mother's dying. My mind was filled with the thought that I should have spent more time with them, have got more emotionally involved, and should have created a greater bond of warmth and friendship and thereby helped them more effectively. When the family eventually arrived, I was surprised when one of the children came up to me and simply embraced me. She said nothing. That simple act gave me the strength to take the service and made me realise that, maybe, I had been of help.

To the pastoral care of those going through bereavement you may bring your own experience and insights, especially if your own mother or father died when you were in your teens. This can be something of great value. However, it is important to remember that your bereavement was just that – *your* bereavement. Understanding the young person's feelings through your own experience must not be allowed to inhibit those feelings. People react to death in ways that can be identified, but within that broad category there will be a wide variety of unique and personal reactions.

Within the framework of accepted bereavement care, what are the emotions that confront someone who is bereaved?

Denial

Coming to terms with a new and unexpected reality can at first be very difficult. The usual emotional response to sudden death, or to news that a loved one is dying, is that of denial – a feeling that 'this cannot be happening to me. It is not true. There must be a mistake'. Initially there may even be a refusal to believe what has happened. This can be a problem if the young person refuses to accept eventually what is reality.

Obviously the nature of the feeling of denial will manifest itself in different ways according to the circumstances that a teenager has been confronted with. If a young person said goodbye when dad went off to work and then is confronted by the news, on getting home from school, that father dropped dead at work, his emotions will be different from those of the teenager who discovers that his already sick mother is dying of cancer.

Anyone who is showing care towards young people should allow them to voice what they feel and gently encourage them to face up to reality and the changed circumstances involved in that. When people begin to accept and face up to what has happened, they are enabled to handle it and grow through the experience.

Anger

'Why me?' may be part of the anger that is felt in such circumstances. For mother or father to die will obviously radically change the environment at home. This will affect young people in all things, from the simple domestic matters right through to the emotional support they may find themselves deprived of. There will be feelings of genuine pity for their parent as well as for themselves. Anger may be what they feel – part of the bitterness toward how badly they have been dealt with by life and by circumstances beyond their control. That anger may be directed towards one target or a number of targets – the doctors, the hospital, the Church or God. This can be very difficult for you to deal with, as a youth leader, because it is strenuous to get alongside someone who is angry – particularly if you are on the receiving end of the anger. If that anger is also laced with a strong degree of bitterness and cynicism, then it is difficult for you to respond to it. Fear can also play its part since the bereaved person may be afraid of being unable to cope. Fear about the future and what it may bring can very easily produce what, on the surface, manifests itself as anger.

Part of your ability to cope will be recognising that anger is part of the bereavement process and that you do not have to have all the answers to the bereaved person's questions. In talking to teenagers under this affliction, it is important to enter into the world of what they are feeling, to try and get emotionally alongside them. In itself, it can be a powerful support for them to know that someone can identify with what they feel.

Bargaining

If a young person is confronted by the imminent or eventual death of mother or father, part of the emotional response will be that of 'bargaining', as the experts have termed it. The person may try to do something or take a course of action as a way of saying, 'If I do this, you must make my mother better'. From a Christian perspective, it can often take the form of bargaining with God. 'If God saves my Dad, then I'll be good for the rest of my life.' This reaction is an emotional way of coping with what is happening and trying to control it. The sad thing is that often Christian communities unconsciously operate in this way by adopting an attitude which affirms that 'if we pray enough and have enough faith, the person will be healed'. Miracle cures do happen; but the reality is that they are not the common experience. The even greater tragedy is when you see a church praying and believing that a person will be healed, and then that person dies, and the church is unable to cope with that and rejects the family because its theology cannot tolerate failure.

We all like to be in control of our lives and the circumstances around us. This is true for adults as well as for teenagers. However, when a dimension is brought into our lives where we lose control, that is very threatening, and the natural human way of trying to re-establish control is this process of bargaining in an attempt to influence what is happening. In a sense it is making ourselves the 'cause' so that we are able to create an 'effect'. If we do something, then it might produce the effect we want.

In talking to teenagers you may find that they will make all sorts of promises of what they will do and be, if only Dad won't die. Such a reaction is normal. However, as a caring youth leader, you must gently and sensitively encourage them to have a balanced perception of reality. A crucial part of the Christian understanding of life is that the ultimate healing is death and resurrection. It is over this wonderful truth that God has complete control.

Sadness, depression

With the death of a parent a significant part of a young person's emotional stability is taken away. The bereaved have lost someone whom they loved, and while they may not have been markedly appreciative of the parent when alive, there will be a tremendous sense of loss. That huge loss will produce sadness and depression which it will take months, and sometimes years, to recover from. The surviving parent, moreover, may be too caught up in his or her own grief to be able to comfort their teenagers. This is where you as a youth leader and part of a Chrsitian community should be able to help. The Gospel message of eternal life has a significant contribution to make to a person's understanding and ability to come to terms with what has happened. However, it is imperative that we don't come out with soft platitudes but properly understand and identify with the sense of loss for the young person, and also offer a cause for hope. Identifying with the person will be a painful process because it will expose us to our own feelings of pain and suffering. But this is a necessary part of our experience if we are to be a genuine help to others. The person who says 'come on, cheer up' is probably refusing to face the cost of caring and will be ineffective in the pastoral role.

For many people who have been bereaved a frequent comment is that they are 'taking one day at a time'. This can be a simple and effective way of coping with the sadness and loss, the reason being that it gives the person a manageable goal. It is interesting that Viktor Frankl, in his book *Man's Search for Meaning*, refers to the fact that, while in a Nazi concentration camp, he observed that the prisoners who survived were usually those who set themselves a goal. This provided an inner strength and something to which they could look forward. Frankl remarks: 'The prisoner who had lost faith in the future – his future – was doomed . . . he let himself decline and became subject to mental and physical decay.'

It will be helpful, in talking to your teenagers, to make gentle enquiry into what personal goals they may be able to set to help see them through their present experiences. It is important to help them choose something which they feel positive about, and which will not add to the pressures on them. To have an aim, and to avoid falling into an unhealthy self-pity, should assist them in not being overwhelmed by their tragedy.

Part of the sadness will inevitably be bound up with the struggle to try and make some sense out of what has happened. This will impinge itself upon the bereaved at all sorts of levels, from 'Why did mum have to die?' to 'Why do I have to come home from school to a cold and lonely house?'

Special times become tinged with sadness. The teenager's birthday, Christmas and holidays are not the same and, unfortunately, never will be. Life has changed and it can be very difficult and depressing for a young person to cope with that. There will need to be a reorientation of life, from the small details of domestic arrangements which mum or dad used to take care of, through to the status of being a child with no mum or dad.

Mixed in with the sadness there is often, as we have noted already, a sense of guilt. The teenager may recall arguments and rows with the deceased parent, and may now feel remorse and recrimination about what was said or done while the parent was alive. Such feelings need to be discussed, aired and worked through. If the sense of guilt is acute, professional help may need to be sought.

Acceptance

Acceptance is generally regarded as the final phase in the bereavement process. The person comes to terms with the loss and is able to cope with the implication of it. However, people vary greatly, as anyone who is regularly involved in family bereavement will tell you. The speed of recovery depends on the individual. A person's ability to come to terms with what has happened will in some senses be unique to that person.

For one experienced youth leader this was particularly highlighted by two girls in his group. The father of one of the girls had committed suicide in very traumatic circumstances. In addition her mother was going blind. The pressures on the young girl were immense, particularly as the family were not financially well-off. But Clare showed great strength and determination within her unhappy circumstances, and those who met her were often unaware of all the trauma she had to cope with. By contrast, Sarah had lost her father when he suddenly died at work. He was in his late forties, a successful businessman who had made more than adequate financial provision for his family. Despite a lot of support, Sarah found it very difficult to come to terms with what had happened, and would frequently burst into tears at the slightest provocation. She would let everyone know that she had lost her father and would use that as a defence if she felt under any pressure.

People vary greatly, and although acceptance is regarded as the final stage in coping with death, these things are rarely as neat and tidy as we would hope. Sometimes all of these stages can be part of the confused emotions that someone feels when facing up to a tragic loss.

In this chapter we have been particularly focusing on the loss of mother or father. But, of course, you may be confronted with teenagers who are mourning the death of one of their friends. A young person may be killed in a motor bike accident or car crash, or die of a disease. You may have to give counselling to teenagers on a group basis. Take care, also, to keep an eye on the friends of someone who is bereaved. They may need help because they are unable to cope with what their friend has experienced. You may also need to make sure that the other teenagers, from fear of not knowing what to say or do, do not isolate the young person who has been bereaved. It is always very sad to hear someone make the reproach that they lost their friends when their spouse died because their friends could not cope with what had happened. This is quite common, as a youth leader you will need to keep an eye on the dynamics of the group and to be aware how the other teenagers are responding to the new and difficult situation.

* It is also important to make sure the grieving process is not going wrong. The manifestation of grief that is unhealthy is when there is either severe depression, guilt or anger. In this case you should refer to a professional counsellor. It is also important to recognise your own limitations and to take care to protect yourself emotionally, and your family if you have one.

Finally, your role will be very important in sharing with the young people their feelings, encouraging them, listening, and simply giving them that love and support they will so very much need.

SUGGESTIONS FOR FURTHER READING

I. Ainsworth-Smith and P. Speck, *Letting Go* (Society for Promoting Christian Knowledge).
Pat Wynne-Jones, *Children, Death and Bereavement* (Scripture Union).

17

UNEMPLOYMENT

Unemployment is one of the most acute social problems facing our society at the end of the twentieth century. Because of the complexity of the issue, all one can do here is to hightlight, and be aware of, some of the problems and pressures that confront a young person out of work.

A psychologist, Dr Donovan, has shown that unemployed young people display a greater number of psychological symptoms – such as anxiety, depression, low self-esteem, physical malaise, anti-social behaviour, abuse of alcohol and drugs – than do those who have a job or are in a training scheme.

Professor Martin Herbert rightly comments that there is no panacea for mitigating the corrosive effects of prolonged unemployment on the morale of adolescents. However, it is possible to be aware of the effect of unemployment and of ways in which you as a youth leader can help pastorally those older teenagers who are out of work and may be facing the prospect of long-term unemployment.

THE PRESSURES

The feelings and pressures that can be identified with unemployment are in one sense common problems linked with difficulties, but in another sense have a distinctive element.

Depression

Having a job is an adult status symbol. A job is equated with being grown up. If young people lose their job or are not given

116

the opportunity to work, it can be a very difficult and depressing experience for them to struggle to discover their own identity. E. Erikson, in his book *Youth Identity and Crisis*, remarks that 'the inability to settle on an occupational identity can be one of the most disturbing problems for young people.'

The emphasis within society is to see the worth of an individual in terms of his or her job. People make value judgements about class and occupation according to a person's function. Take away the function and individuals lose their status in society and their self-esteem. You, as a youth leader, will have a positive pastoral role to play because, as the *Faith in the City* report said, 'the Church must affirm that each of us is valued by God, in whose image we are made, for ourselves – and not for what we do' (9:110).

Young people may feel that they are just another statistic in the dole queue figures or that they have been thrown on the scrap-heap before they have even had the opportunity to prove themselves and make a contribution to society. It can be immensely difficult to adjust to not having the spending power to go and buy the recent record release or the clothes you want. The lack of money greatly affects what you can go out and do. The pub is too expensive and many forms of adolescent enjoyment are beyond the financial means of the young unemployed. All this paints a very depressing picture for the out-of-work young person.

Anger and frustration

Many young people in their search for a real job have written literally hundreds of letters of application. Mostly they get no reply. Every letter sent is in many ways carrying something of the person in it. It carries hope and a preparation to offer oneself to do something. Each reply saying No, even a lack of acknowledgment, is a statement of not being wanted, of rejection. To have one's hopes continually dashed can be extremely depressing and a frustrating experience. A lot of teenagers feel angry at the government and disillusioned with the organisations that are supposed to help.

Insecurity and uncertainty

Not to have a role or function is a very difficult experience. To add to that the uncertainties about your own value and your own future creates a situation immensely difficult to come to terms with. There are some within society who face the prospect of *never* actually 'working' in terms of a job in the traditional sense. The lack of prospects for a young person creates insecurity around marriage, family, housing and actually ever managing to achieve something in life. How can you make plans when you have no opportunity to create any sort of future?

Parents

Many teenagers experience difficulties from the pressure exerted by their parents. The problems involved with someone always being at home and around are obvious. Teenagers at times keep up an appearance of just not caring or even being cheerful in the face of unemployment. This leads to parents feeling that their teenager is not bothered to motivate himself to get a job. If you can encourage your unemployed young person to talk with their parents and express what they are feeling, you can thereby do a lot to lessen the building up of pressure at home.

Parents naturally are emotionally involved with the well-being of their teenagers and can feel helpless, frustrated, angry and despairing about them. Without a job, a young person's dependence on the family home is increased at precisely the time when he or she would be developing a more independent life-style. All the emotions that go with being without a job will not only affect the morale, motivation and personal discipline of the individual, but will also have a general impact on family life as a whole.

Racial discrimination

Sadly, it is evident that a white boy or girl stands a better chance of getting a job than someone of a different racial background.

This point is referred to in the *Faith in the City* report (at 9:20) of the General Synod.

WAYS OF HELPING UNEMPLOYED TEENAGERS IN YOUR GROUP

- Assist them to deal constructively with the problems facing them.
- Encourage them to see that their value as individuals lies primarily in who they are and not in what they do.
- Help them in form-filling and job applications.
- Be aware of local schemes for the unemployed, and find out what job-training projects are available.
- Encourage them to look at the possibilities for further education. A better qualified person is better placed to get a job.
- Provide general encouragement and support for them to continue job-hunting, especially when they are experiencing new disappointments in their efforts.
- Suggest they look into the possibility of seeking a job further afield, and ask them to consider if it would help to move away from home.
- Look into the opportunities for voluntary community service.
- See if there is any opportunity for people with their skills to become self-employed. (The Prince's Trust may be of help.)
- Contact your local councillors or MP, who may be aware of agencies that can help.
- Encourage them to re-examine job types which they had previously thought unsuitable.
- Contact the local Trade Unions. They may be able to offer help and advice.
- Encourage them to make the most of the time they have available to develop new interests and personal skills.
- Help them to maintain a sense of normality about their lives.
- Help them to develop a positive self-image.

SUGGESTIONS FOR FURTHER READING

W. Green, *The Church and Unemployment* (Mowbray).
National Youth Agency – publishes a number of useful
booklets on work with young unemployed, 17–23
Albion Street, Leicester LE1 6GD. Tel. 0533 471200.

RESOURCES

Prince's Trust, 8 Bedford Row, London WC1R 4BA.

18
DRUGS

Most people are aware that drug abuse is a growing problem. Each year new statistics produced over a whole range of drug-abuse issues show that the numbers involved are increasing. The average age of those cautioned or prosecuted is 26, but there is evidence that the problem is developing among the lower age range of late childhood and early teenage.

But what are we talking about when we refer to drug abuse? For the purpose of this chapter we will refer only to those drugs that are illegal. Substances such as alcohol and tobacco are, of course, drugs and if you refer to chapter 28, on Young People and the Law, you can see the legal implications. However, tobacco and alcohol do not come under the Misuse of Drugs Act of 1971.

If you as a youth leader have not had a case of drug involvement then you are very fortunate. Part of the problem is that we live in a drug-orientated society. Some of the parents of your teenagers will be very familiar with anti-depressants, tranquillisers and sleeping pills. Drugs are common and frequently prescribed as an answer to an emotional or physical problem. This is the beneficial medical side of drugs. Yet if you talk to your local policeman, and particularly the drugs officer, he will tell you of the pubs in the area that are known as places where drugs can be obtained. Moreover, some of the schools or sixth-form colleges may be places where a certain amount of abuse is taking place. This serves to illustrate the point that the world of drugs is our world and the world of our young people.

Involvement of teenagers in drug abuse will usually be through friends at their points of social contact. They may do it to experiment, as part of the risk-taking process, or because they are depressed. Teenagers take drugs for a variety of reasons. Often it starts off as something to do for fun or to relieve stress, and because of the nature of drugs they become hooked.

The best way for you as a youth leader to help prevent drug abuse among the teenagers with whom you have contact is, firstly, to be informed of the nature of the substances; secondly, to be aware of what the general situation is in the local area; and, thirdly, to know where to get advice and assistance.

DRUG TERMS

Dependence

This is the word used for the compulsion to continue taking a drug as a result of repeated administration. Two terms are used: 'Physical Dependence', which takes place to avoid the physical discomfort of withdrawal; and 'Psychological Dependence', which refers to the need for stimulation and pleasure. It is widely regarded that psychological dependence is the most widespread and difficult problem.

Tolerance

People develop a tolerance, so that eventually the body will adapt to the high quantity of any drug. The problem then, of course, is that a higher quantity of the drug is needed to obtain the same effect.

Withdrawal

This refers to the effect upon the body when a drug is suddenly absent to which it has become adapted. Such an experience can be extremely painful, and it may take up to two or three weeks for the body to adjust. Of course, a fresh intake of the drug will alleviate the immediate problem.

Addiction

This refers to the fact that drug dependency has developed into a serious problem which has effects on the individual and society.

DRUG ABUSE AND THE LAW

One result of drug abuse may be involvement in criminal offences. The Misuse of Drugs Act 1971 divides drugs in three classes – A, B and C. Class A carries the most serious punishment and includes drugs such as heroin, cocaine and LSD. Class B contains cannabis resin and certain barbiturates and amphetamines (although these can become Class A if prepared for injection). Class C contains other drugs in the amphetamine group.

Further and possibly more extensive criminal activity may result from entry into the illegal world of drugs. Cheating, stealing, burglary, prostitution and dealing in illegal drugs may all be used to finance the habit. It is often assumed that users will also tend to become more aggressive and that they may more easily be involved in hostile acts such as mugging, sexual abuse and violence within the family. Opiates, which show the most rapid increase in use, are heavy sedative-type drugs and likely to produce the opposite of anger or violence. Drugs such as barbiturates can reduce inhibition in the same way that alcohol does in those who may have aggressive tendencies.

First offenders who are charged with the possession of drugs only for their own use will probably be fined; but they will still have a criminal record. Regular offenders, however, may be imprisoned. The maximum for trafficking offences is fourteen years in prison. Young people between the ages of ten and sixteen are usually dealt with in the Juvenile Court.

Any parent or individual who comes into possession of a substance he thinks is illegal should hand it into the police immediately.

HELPING THOSE INVOLVED IN DRUGS

A minor involvement with illegal drugs may be handled quietly and reasonably between you and the parents of the young person involved. If you can develop a positive relationship with both the teenager and the parents you may be able to stop the use of cannabis, for example. However, if the dependence on drugs is of a more serious nature, you need to proceed with great care, recognising that you should be only part of the means by which a young person comes to terms with the problem and seeks help. Other professional sources need to be mobilised to overcome the problem.

If it is right for you to become involved, or indeed if your help is sought because of the circumstances concerned, then do not preach. Rather, your attitude needs to be one of care and real concern for the person. You will need to gain the confidence of the teenagers. The degree to which you can play your part in helping them will depend on the quality of your relationship with them. It is important to listen and understand, and to offer support and reassurance. You may need to talk sensitively with them to discover the emotional reasons for their dependence on a drug. Was it because of pressure of school work and parental expectations, or because they have a low self-esteem? If you can reach beneath the surface of the drug problem, you will be able to counsel and help them handle the deeper issues involved. They may need to be encouraged to change their life-style and develop new interests which absorb their time and energy. Also a new circle of friends will need to be encouraged so that they can get away from those who have access to the drugs and are influencing the teenager's dependence.

It is important to remember that, if you do seek to help a young person, it may be at a considerable cost to yourself. It may involve a great deal of your time and certainly a lot of your emotional energy. Some drug users become pathological and may steal from you. They may be prepared to take all that you can offer them and more, and when they have done that they may throw it all back in your face. You need to exercise a balance of care and realistic assessment. There is no room for naivety.

Finally, we must recognise that we are not experts even if we are well-informed about the facts of drugs and their misuse. As I have said, we need to see ourselves as part of the solution to a person's drug dependence. We must be ready to seek professional medical, psychiatric and social advice. Family doctors and voluntary groups have a crucial role to play.

It is important to our helping teenagers that we should be aware of the signs of drug use. The concluding section of this chapter, on Signs and Symptoms, gives specific details of the effects of different types of drugs. For convenience, however, I also list below some of the more obvious general signs you should look for. You will, of course, notice that some of the signs are such that parents will be better placed to recognise them, and also that some of the indications are general adolescent characteristics. This all emphasises the fact that it is not easy to recognise misuse. As a youth leader you are probably more likely to be aware of the problem through information that comes to you about the presence of drugs at school or at the pub. So, look out for the following, present separately or combined:

- a general lethargy
- sudden changes of mood
- uncharacteristic aggression
- poor physical appearance
- loss of interest in school work, friends, food, hobbies
- A change of personal habits
- frequent lying
- speech becoming slow
- money disappearing
- periods of sleeplessness or of drowsiness
- unusual 'phone calls or strange messages
- unexpected departure
- unexpected disappearance
- spots of blood on clothing
- needle marks on body

IN AN EMERGENCY

In emergency situations (overdose, bad withdrawal symptoms, etc), do not hesitate to dial 999 and ask for an ambulance, stating which drugs (and/or alcohol) may be involved.

While waiting for the emergency service to arrive, keep the person warm but with plenty of space and ventilation.

Do not attempt to move him or her, but try to position in the following First Aid emergency position: Lay the person on one side (underneath arm placed comfortably behind the body) with the upper arm bent, so that the forearm forms a pillow for the forehead.

Tilt the head so that the mouth and nose are pointing towards the floor.

From time to time make sure that the mouth is open and not obstructed by the tongue or vomit.

DRUG-USE SIGNS AND SYMPTOMS

1 *Amphetamines, stimulants, cocaine*

CLINICAL NAMES Benzedrine, Dexedrine, Drinamyl, Durophet, Ritalin, Preludin, etc.

STREET NAMES Uppers, blue, dominoes, block bombers, minstrels, speed, meth, pep-pills.
  Cocaine: Sweets, C, Charlie, Coke.

SYMPTOMS Users feel more alert, energetic, confident, cheerful or less bored, less tired. Increase of heart-rate, breathing; pupils dilate; loss of appetite, insomnia, bad breath and mouth ulcers. Some may feel anxious, restless, irritable or dizzy. *Large doses:* delirium, panic, hallucinations or feelings of persecution.

  Cocaine: Symptoms show similar effects. Generally a feeling of great physical strength and mental capacity. Effects wear off quicker than with amphetamines. *Large doses:* erratic or violent behaviour, agitation or anxiety. Possible hallucinations.

DANGERS No true addiction but great reluctance to stop because of the stimulating effects. Tolerance to the drugs very rapid, therefore dosage rapidly increased. *Regular or high doses:* low resistance to disease, heart palpitations, liver and kidney malfunction; brain function may be affected. Dramatic ageing. Feelings of persecution may lead to acts of hostility;

psychotic state may develop. *Regular or high doses:* similar feelings of persecution, unpleasant skin sensations. Euphoria replaced by unpleasant reactions – nausea, restlessness, etc. Sniffing can damage nose membranes. Injections can cause abscesses long-term. Impure injections can be fatal.

WITHDRAWAL Deep feelings of depression and fatigue. No obvious physical symptoms.

2 Tranquillisers

CLINICAL NAMES Librium, Valium, Oblivon, Equanil, Ativan, Dalmane.

STREET NAMES Sleepers.

SYMPTOMS Depresses mental activity and alertness. Relaxes muscles, sedates and reduces anxiety. Can lead to drowsiness, lethargy and forgetfulness. *Adverse reactions:* lack of co-ordination, skin eruptions, constipation, nausea, jaundice. In some cases may release aggression.

DANGERS Psychological dependence – users feel unable to cope without them. Tolerance to the drugs very rapid, leading to increases of dosage and danger of physical dependence. *Overdose:* has to be large quantity to be fatal – but fatality possible, especially if combined with alcohol.

WITHDRAWAL Can cause insomnia, anxiety, distortion of time, tremors, nausea, vomiting. High doses may produce convulsions and mental confusion. These can be alleviated by more gradual withdrawal.

3 Depressants, barbiturates

CLINICAL NAMES Amytal, nembutal, seconal, tuinal, soneryl, sodium amytal, pentothal, luminal, largactil, physeptone, stelazine. Welldorm, doriden, mogadon, methaqualone, mandrax.

STREET NAMES Sleepers, downers, barba; mandies (for mandrax).

SYMPTOMS Drugs depress central nervous system. Similar effects to overuse of alcohol. *Small doses:* feeling of relaxation, social ability, good humour. *Large doses:* clumsiness, poor control of speech and body, therefore liable to accidental injury.

May be aggressive if combined with alcohol. Drowsiness, staggering, lack of interest and feeling of disorientation.

DANGERS Strong physical and psychological dependence. Tolerance to the drugs is very rapid. Addiction easily created by a regular pattern or taking the drugs so many times a week – more so if taken daily. Heavy users prone to pneumonia and hypothermia, especially if injecting, which is more dangerous than oral use. Suicide and accidental death alarmingly high, especially if mixing with alcohol or sleeping pills. Number of tablets for fatal dosage is often not very high. Danger of unconsciousness and respiratory failure. Withdrawal dangers as below.

WITHDRAWAL Irritability, nervousness, insomnia, weakness, headaches, anxiety, followed by shaking, nausea, vomiting, stomach cramps, convulsions. Delirium or hallucinations possible. If sudden, withdrawal can be fatal. Fits and convulsions can cause lasting brain damage.

4 *Opiates*

CLINICAL NAMES Heroin, morphine, diconal, pethidine, opium, methadone, codeine.

STREET NAMES Jack, junk, smack, horse, H (for heroin), M (for morphine). *Methods:* 'chasing the dragon' (sniffing); 'mainlining' (injecting).

SYMPTOMS *First users* (especially injecting): nausea and vomiting common. *Continuous use:* affects nervous system, including reflex functions of coughing, respiration and heart-rate. Feelings of warmth due to dilation of blood vessels. Contraction of pupils, constipation; speech may be slow and slurred. Most experience drowsiness, a feeling of well-being and contentment. Euphoria – with relaxed detachment from pain, anxiety, desire for food, sex etc. Apathy – leading to neglect of hygiene and nutrition, to bad housing conditions etc.; users therefore prone to other infections and diseases.

DANGERS Psychological or social dependence very strong. Physical dependence not as significant – some can use heroin on an occasional basis.

Sniffing can lead to damage of nose tissue; impurities can lead to respiratory disease. *Injection* can lead to bad scars, especially with unhygienic methods and impure heroin; impurities can be fatal. *Swallowing* is safest method; less predictable and slower in effect.

Large dosage: can lead to stupor or coma.

WITHDRAWAL Difficult – with aches, tremors, sweating, chills, sneezing, yawning, muscular spasms, for 7–10 days. Weakness lasts for several months. Many users slip back after treatment.

5 Hallucinogens

CLINICAL NAMES Mescaline, LSD, psilocybin, IOM, STP, phencyclidine, hallucinogenic amphetamines, hallucinogenic mushrooms.

STREET NAMES Acid, brand names such as 'white lightning'.

SYMPTOMS For LSD: alters perception of time and space. Usual effects – intensifying of colours, sizes and shapes; stationary objects perceived as moving. Feeling of dissociation from the body (tripping). Changes in mood and behaviour, lessening of inhibitions. Dilated pupils. Body temperature and blood pressure can also be affected.

For Mushrooms: as above, but more prominent euphoria or hilarity. Physical signs – heart-rate, blood pressure and size of pupils more obvious.

High doses: can progress to vivid visual hallucinations, but the mind remains alert. (This is disputed by some.)

DANGERS No physical dependence. Effectiveness of LSD doses diminishes with frequent use, therefore discouraging regular use. No reliable evidence of long-term brain damage. No known cases of overdose. Main danger is psychological. Anxiety, bad trips and short trips may cause distress or disorientation. Suicide or death as direct result of LSD perceptions is rare.

6 *Cannabis, marijuana*

STREET NAMES Grass, dope, pot, hash, reefers, joints, smoke, spliffs, tea, weed, resin.

SYMPTOMS Talkativeness, bouts of hilarity, relaxation, greater appreciation of sound and colour. *Large doses:* distortion in awareness of time, changes in visual perception (eyes may be bloodshot); forgetfulness, hunger and thirst, lack of concentration, distorted judgement. User may become drowsy, especially when effects wear off. Sometimes may lead to hostile behaviour.

DANGERS No physical dependence, but users may rely on the drug for psychological or social needs. No hangover or danger of overdose. No conclusive evidence of lasting damage to physical or mental health (further study necessary on this). Frequent inhalation can cause bronchitis or other respiratory disorders, possibly lung cancer. User may withdraw from society. Greatest danger is the frequency of users progressing to 'harder' drugs.

7 *Delirants, solvents*

CLINICAL NAMES Contact adhesives, glue, nail-varnish remover, cleaning fluid, surgical spirit, shoe conditioner, paint thinner, anti-freeze, petrol, rubber solution, typewriter correction-fluid and thinners. Aerosols, deodorants, gas-lighter fuel.

SYMPTOMS Glazed looks, boils around mouth, red ring around nose, pallor. Fatigue, apparent drunkenness, with inability to stand or walk properly. Lack of understanding and irrational behaviour. Interest in food may diminish. Smell of glue or chemicals on clothing. Much time spent away from home, poor attendance at school/college/work. These symptoms are found in the more serious cases of sniffing.

Those not so involved may exhibit only a few signs, such as sores on the face, glazed look, smelling of glue or chemicals.

DANGERS No evidence of long-term addiction; tends to be short-term problem. Possible damage, in longer term, to vital organs from some of the chemicals. Awareness, judgement and reactions become impaired – proneness, therefore, to accidents and physical injuries. Direct death is rare, although user can choke on vomit or suffocate in plastic bag. Sniffing may often be done in dangerous places.

19
SEX

CARE OF YOUNG PEOPLE IN SEXUAL MATTERS

Everyone is aware that we live in an age that is extremely sexually conscious. If sex was a taboo subject in the last century, that has been made up for by the explosion of sexuality in the latter part of the twentieth century. Our young people are growing up in a world where sex is high on the agenda items of experience and practice. The 'James Bond' image is a strong expression of society's attitude to the nature and role of sex.

Sex is used in advertising. It is portrayed on television, in magazines and films. For many teenagers sex magazines will be circulating around school; and with the widespread sales of videos, soft and hard pornography can be viewed at home. The current myth that everyone is doing it is reinforced by the media, and many girls are led to believe they will never have boyfriends unless they are prepared to go to bed with them.

Approximately 1 in 4 children are born out of wedlock. Cohabitation has lost its stigma and is a common social phenomenon. In Leslie Francis' survey of Christian young people in the age range of sixteen to twenty, only 35 per cent agreed with the statement that they thought it was wrong to have sexual intercourse outside marriage.

If sex is high on the agenda for society, it is crucial that it should also be prominent in the teaching of the Church. However, the truth is that even Christian teenagers receive very little of their knowledge about sex from a Christian source. This was highlighted by the series of articles in *Buzz* magazine in 1987, entitled 'Twentieth Century Sex'. This highly controversial series was an attempt to give a Christian perspective on issues of sexual activity which affect today's young people.

The main sources of information about sex are through school, the media and other teenagers. Few parents feel that they can discuss sex with their teenagers, which is unfortunate because those young people who do take a responsible attitude are those who have been well-instructed and who have the opportunity to discuss the subject openly and positively.

School sex education has been frequently criticised as giving an unbalanced view of sex with its concentration on the physical side of intercourse. Professor Martin Herbert remarks:

> Most regrettable of all (some would maintain) is the fact that sex can be compartmentalised, separated from all the other needs, aspirations, attitudes and feelings with which it is usually inextricably interwoven in the psychological make-up of the mature individual. If sex is a thing rather than a loving relationship, it can be switched off and on; being sexually aroused then simplifies to finding an attractive sex object.

The Church has a real and vital role in its teaching and pastoral support of individuals as they explore and work out their own sexuality. As far back as 1929, Pius XI in his encyclical on the Christian Education of Youth emphasised the wholeness of man, soul united to body, and the need for the minds of children to be imbued with teaching that comes from God and is filled with divine grace. The youth leader will be part of that education since adolescence is a time when those powerful feelings emerge. The issues of emotional and biological development I have looked at in chapters 10 and 11, on Adolescence and on Puberty. Young people today are confronted by the maturity of their own sexuality at an earlier stage than their parents, and the evidence is that sexual experience is becoming more common among youngsters in their later childhood and early teenage years.

The consequences of ignoring the development of a positive Christian attitude towards sex among the young people in your club, youth group or fellowship should be obvious enough. One church group which had strongly emphasised general spiritual and biblical teaching, while ignoring relationships and sexuality, found that many of its teenagers were involved in casual sex. This was not surprising! Young people will know of pupils at school who will be having abortions. There is the question of the effect on the group when a young girl starts coming along who has a baby at home to take care of. As a youth leader you probably have at least a handful of present and past pastoral situations which are connected with sexual activity. If you haven't you are probably ignorant about what really is happening among your teenagers. Or you look after a group of perfect angels.

Relationships and sex should be on the agenda of issues raised and openly discussed among Christian young people. However, there are two important steps to be taken before such issues are raised and treated as an on-going part of the pastoral care of the young.

Firstly, you need to bring your priest or pastor into extensive consultation.

You may not agree with everything your clergy hold with on these issues, especially since the Church's interpretation of the Biblical teaching is not universally consistent. But you will need the support and understanding of the clergy if you are to raise these sensitive issues under the umbrella of the teachings of the Church.

Secondly, you need to be comfortable with your own feelings about the various aspects that are involved in the subject of sex. This is simply because sex is not an easy subject to handle; it can bring to the surface strong emotions and at times feelings of guilt. To be able to talk openly and frankly about sex requires a good deal of knowledge, self-awareness, courage and sensitivity. You may find it helpful to discriminate between (*a*) what you feel, (*b*) what you think, and (*c*) what you know concerning certain sexual issues.

As an exercise for yourself, the other youth leaders or your clergy, you may wish to discuss:

- Pre-marital sex.
- Casual sex.
- Virginity.
- Pornography.
- Child abuse.

First of all, discuss one or all of the subjects from the perspective of what you *feel* about the issues involved. In other words – what is your 'gut reaction', and what experiences trigger that reaction? Then, secondly, go on to talk about the subject from the viewpoint of what you *think* about it. This will involve your opinions and the stand you take over the issues. Thirdly, what is your knowledge of the facts. As you discuss around the subject, you may become aware that you do not know all the facts, or even the names of various parts of the body and their function. Having a full awareness of the facts is essential, and that may even change or modify what you believe. You may find that you are unsure of some of your beliefs about sexual matters simply because you lack some of the facts relating to the subject. Often people get confused between what is their feeling about something, and what is their opinion and knowledge of the facts. If you can separate these three aspects it will help you to come to terms in a fuller way with the various dimensions of sex and will help you in handling the issue in relation to other people.

As Lance Pierson points out in his book *Sex and Young People*, 'The Church is generally perceived as taking a negative view of sex and being something of a kill-joy. The Christian view of sex needs to be restored to a positive attitude which esteems the rich expression of sex and part of the value and meaning for each individual.'

In attempting to foster a Christian view, what should the youth leader be attempting to do as an overall policy? I suggest five things:

1 Provide the biological facts. (First you have got to know them.)
2 Develop the understanding of sex within the context of

emotional, psychological, moral, social and spiritual growth, in yourself and others.

3 Explode the various myths and fears about sex (such as masturbation is harmful and can make you go mad, blind, impotent or stunt your growth). Learning the facts can explode the myths.

4 Encourage an informed and positive view of human and individual sexuality.

5 Sexuality is natural and good. What is important is what we do with it. Inform the young people of the consequences involved in sexual activity and offer practical advice where needed.

How do you go about actually putting this into practice, even assuming you have followed through all that has been said so far and is outlined above? If you are a couple running a group, then you should feel competent to do things if you have worked out your own sexuality. If not, invite another couple or individual to come and discuss the matter. You may feel ill-equipped to talk corporately to the group, but you may be happy to pick up the issues raised and discussed in a more informal basis.

If you are a single person running the group without any additional help, then you may be best advised not to raise the issue yourself but to invite a competent outsider. If I may give a piece of general advice, I would suggest that you do not automatically invite a married couple to speak on the issue to your teenagers. It is well and good for a couple to express the Christian view of sex and marriage, but many of the young people may feel – 'Well, it's okay for them, they are married'. I made the mistake of undervaluing my contribution as a single person when I was invited to preach at a youth service in a big church in the south-east of England. When I received the invitation to preach on 'Sex and Marriage', I immediately wrote back to the vicar asking if he realised that I was not married? His reply was that he especially wanted a single person because an unmarried speaker would have more of an understanding of the pressures upon individuals who are trying to live out a Christian life-style as a single person. In fact, whether single or married, all of us have to work out our own boundaries and views, and these are often constantly under examination.

Finally, as a youth leader avoid being on your own when counselling a teenager of either sex, particularly when dealing with sexual matters. Such a practice is a recipe for possible disaster. If you are married, try to involve your husband or wife. If you are single, it will help if there is present someone else who is trusted. You may not think you are the type of person who gets involved with a younger girl or boy; but the fact is, it happens. Young people can fall in love with youth leaders, particularly if there has been close emotional sharing. You may find that rather flattering or even tempting! With counselling it is important to have someone else around, if only in the same building. This helps preserve professional ethics and avoids misunderstanding. While rumours may be untrue, the damage that can be done to an individual, church and community is immense. Also, on the more mundane level, such individual counselling sessions can give rise to gossip. So always err on the side of caution!

SOME ISSUES RELEVANT TO TEENAGERS

The range of issues that sex and relationships throw up is enormous, but just some of the talking points will be:

- What do we mean by sex?
- Is sex before marriage always wrong?
- How far can you go physically with your boyfriend or girlfriend?
- Should you only go out with a Christian?
- How does a girl say no?
- How does a boy say no?
- What is the big deal in being a virgin?
- Is masturbation wrong?
- What about your thoughts? (Some experts reckon that

male adolescents think about sex every fifty seconds.)
How do individuals handle their thoughts in the light of
Jesus' teachings in Matthew 5:27 & 28?
● How do you handle guilt about sex?

Part of the human process of growing up is to do with taking
risks. Teenagers will often be motivated by sexual curiosity
and may take risks in developing their experience and human
awareness. In fact, curiosity about your own body begins at
birth. School sex education has as its primary aim the
minimisation of the risks that teenagers take, and aims to make
sure that female adolescents do not get pregnant. However,
we should be dealing with the whole person, and we should
help to minimise any emotional damage as well, so that
individuals grow up with healthy, loving relationships.

HIV/AIDS

Many of the teenagers who you work with will receive teaching
about Human Immunodeficiency Virus (HIV) and Acquired
Immune Deficiency Syndrome (AIDS) from school and the
media. Some of the young people may be pretty tired of hearing
about the issue. However, even though they may be reasonably
well informed about the virus the question of the Christian
moral response may surface from time to time.

If you as a leader are not fully aware of the facts then there
are a variety of publications available from many sources. Two
books which I would recommend are

1 *AIDS and Young People*
2 *The Truth about AIDS*

Both books are written by Dr Patrick Dixon, an acknowledged
expert, and are published by Kingsway.

However while the factual information is easily available is
it possible to sum up some of the moral issues surrounding
AIDS and the Christian response? Firstly, sex is good, but the
place for sexual intercourse is within the framework of a loving
lifelong commitment. Our sexuality is a fundamental part of

our God-given nature, but as with anything of great value it should be handled with care and in the right way. The traditional Christian understanding is that sex has its rightful place with the loving commitment of marriage between husband and wife. However, guidance concerning AIDS needs to take into account the love life of homosexual people and those who are single. You must remember, however, that not all Christians, be they adults or teenagers, believe that sexual intercourse should be just for marriage, but that within a loving stable relationship it is acceptable even if it is between people of the same sex. Secondly, Jesus treated everyone, but particularly the suffering in society, with compassion and loving concern. Any suggestion that AIDS is the punishment of God on an individual is not consistent with biblical teaching. It is rather a matter of cause and effect as opposed to crime and judgement. If you refer to Luke 13:2 and John 9:3 I think it illustrates the point. Thirdly, the Christian message is about God's love which is offered to everyone and that love is stronger than disease and death. The person suffering from AIDS is in need of the news of the love of God just as much as anyone else. We therefore should not treat them with prejudice and fear but with care and understanding.

SUGGESTIONS FOR FURTHER READING

Lance Pierson, *Sex and Young People* (Kingsway Publications).

Michael Lawson and David Skipp, *Sex and That* (Lion Publishing).

Edward Patey, *Christians and Sex* (Mowbray).

Leonore Telfer, *Human Sexuality* (Harper and Row).

'Young People's Attitudes towards Personal and Sexual Attitudes', Research project report available from the National Youth Office, Church House, Westminster, London SW1P 3NZ.

PART THREE

Successful Youth Work

20
LOCATION

What is the best location for your youth group meeting? Is it necessarily the one you are using at the moment? Are you making the best of your facilities?

It is true to say that a good location can help create a good atmosphere in which a group can meet. It is equally true that bad premises can kill the effective work of any club. No one wants to turn up to a place that is cold, dreary and generally depressing.

I remember a number of years ago, going to a disco in a church hall in Kilkenny in the south of Ireland. It was probably one of the dullest parties I have ever been to. I walked into the large hall to be met by a musty damp smell which – combined with the visual presentation of two-tone artillery green walls, where the paint was parting company with the plaster – gave me the impression that I had entered the redundant wing of a Victorian mental hospital. The unattractiveness of the place was increased by the attendance. If the disco had been for two hundred it might have sufficiently filled the hall and given it some atmosphere. However, the thirty people dancing in the corner were the sum total of the folk that evening. Though they worked vigorously to inject some sort of life into the occasion, the evening was a total flop. It was a flop, not because the music was bad or the people lacked life and energy, but because the location was a complete disaster.

Such an example is an extreme case, but it is very common for groups to give little thought to the location they use. People seem to overlook the fact that the drab appearance is working

143

against the warm and friendly atmosphere they are trying to create, simply because they have no alternative place to meet and the group has always met in that hall. The atmosphere is of great importance to any group, and the atmosphere is affected by the location.

If you have got a small group, it is probably best to meet in someone's house. Potentially the atmosphere can be warm and friendly, and it's reasonably easy in a house to create a sense of intimacy and belonging. Serving coffee and chatting to people after the main evening's programme is easy, especially if they are made to feel they can stay and just talk. The importance of a relaxed social time is that it can provide the opportunity for the leaders to get to know their young people.

If you are using a home there are, however, two important points to remember. In the first place, make sure there is a definite time when everyone has to leave. Abusing hospitality is not only discourteous but means you may not be invited back. Recently, a group of older teenagers who went to say goodnight to their hosts discovered they had already gone to bed. Secondly, if it is at all possible be consistent about where you meet. If you meet in a different house each week, this will only serve to break up the group. Some will forget the address and others, due to lack of familiarity, will not bother to come. If it is familiar ground and they know their friends will be there, then you are halfway to making it a good occasion.

Most groups tend to meet in a hall. So next time you go down to open up, look around and ask yourself some of these questions:

- What's your immediate impression of the place?
- What is the state of decoration?
- Does the place need repainting with more attractive colours?
- Is the lighting too dull or too bright?
- Could you use coloured lights?
- Would posters or banners help?
- Could you paint a good mural on one of the walls?

- Is the furniture suitable for the needs of the group?
- Could the hall be sectioned off to create a more viable space?
- Would the atmosphere be helped by some background music during any social time?
- What other ways can the group use to make the place more attractive and welcoming?

Most church halls tend to be rather impersonal, but if you can make your location a place that your teenagers personally identify with in a positive way, then it can make big difference to the social atmosphere. So if the place is in a bad state of decoration, why not get the group to set about a project of repainting? One youth group in Cornwall, which a friend used to run, had never really come together as a group. The leaders always found it a struggle to get any momentum into the activities they were organising. It was only when the members set about redecorating their own premises that the dynamic of the group changed. Because they were working together and doing something of a common interest, the relationships within the group began to work. After they had downed paint pots and brushes, they never looked back. The group took off.

Of course, if you do decide to redecorate the hall, a lot of consultation will have to go on beforehand with those who have responsibility for the premises. If you approach them in the right way and they can see that you have genuine interest in the property, you should have no problem in coming to an agreement.

Lighting is very important. Most homes today have moved away from the single central light that illuminates the whole room. A lot more side and directional lighting is used because people have noticed it creates a softer and more pleasant atmosphere. In halls, however, you often get the glaring white strip-lighting which tends to be very obtrusive; or, at the opposite end of the scale, there is dim, yellow illumination which makes the hall depressing. If you have someone in the congregation with the necessary electrical skills, you can easily install additional lighting which can be used as a secondary system with spotlights and directional lights. Coloured lights can also be used. You may want to consider purchasing or making a portable circuit of coloured light bulbs which can be used in the club or outside when you are having a barbecue in the summer. It helps to give the occasion more of a party atmosphere.

Many churches today have discovered that attractive banners with pictures and a message have dramatically improved the inside appearance of a hall or room which otherwise was cold and undistinguished. Many young people enjoy making banners, and a project to make a number of them, to be hung from the walls of the hall, can be very successful. The inventive and artistic skills of some teenagers come to the fore in such circumstances. What a beautiful effect can be created with a series of colourful banners decorating the walls of an otherwise plain hall!

Another possibility is to use posters. At the moment there are an incredible number of good posters available which can be purchased fairly cheaply. In fact, if you do a survey among your young people you will probably find that a good many have posters on their bedroom walls. Why not ask them to bring them along to the group meeting when they have finished with them?

The other possibility, which will not be feasible for all groups, is to let the teenagers paint a mural or murals of their own on the walls of the club. Some of you may have nightmares at the thought, but it may prove a worthwhile venture. There is a youth club in Surrey which had premises especially built for the teenagers of the local area. After the building was open, for the first two years or so, the attendance was very poor and some serious doubts were raised about its remaining open. But then one of the leaders hit on the idea of inviting all the young people to plan the decorations and paint the place. Permission was granted. Murals were painted and pictures hung which reflected the young people's interests, thoughts and feelings. What the teenagers did was very important; they put their imprint on the club, it became theirs. As a result, the situation changed and it began to attract the people for which it was intended.

A good display board or notice board can be very useful. If, for example, you have recently been away on a trip, or had some social activity, a display board will enable you to show photographs of the trip or the event. Most people like to see themselves, and usually have a good laugh at themselves and each other. A notice board can also display posters of local events and details of future occasions in the group's programme. If any of the young people find themselves in the local paper – let us hope for the best reasons – you can pin up the article. This all helps to create a sense of belonging and identity. You may have often noticed that a guest speaker who is invited to speak about a specific organisation or project may bring his own display board with him. It helps that person to communicate more readily. A good board in a club, therefore, helps to remind the group of the amount of activity that is going on and the fun that can be had.

It may not be a problem for some groups, but for those which have their own rooms or premises furnishing the place satisfactorily can be difficult. If advertising around the church community does not produce results, you could always try approaching a local bank or business firm. Most business organisations renew their office furniture from time to time, and some of the discarded items may be suitable for your group and the premises you use. Try writing to the manager. He may well be able to put you in touch with his firm's depot where its old equipment is stored. Remember, as with most things: if you never ask, you never get!

Another point to consider is space. If the hall is too big for your group, why not section it off with partition boards, or curtains? Create a space that is viable for the group. By using plywood and carpentry skills from the congregation and your group, partitions can readily be constructed. The more mobile they are, the better. If you are going to break up into discussion groups during the evening, it helps greatly if you can easily move partitions to create separate spaces. Or if you want to end with games, you can easily move them to one side.

Finally, there is a small point worth considering when using a hall – music. Have you noticed how friends often have background music playing when you go round for drinks or coffee? Some people find it irritating, I know, but most of us seem to feel that music helps to create a relaxed atmosphere. If you can put together the facilities so that people's favourite music can be played, it helps. But mind you take care that those with obscure tastes in way-out styles don't monopolise the tape deck or record player. That can turn a lot of the others off, particularly if they have to suffer the strains of music which is definitely out of vogue.

21
PROGRAMME PLANNING

A lot of youth groups have a problem with putting together a good programme. This is, indeed, not an easy task; and if you are going to have a good programme there are a number of factors to consider. But before going further, turn back to chapter 1 on Aims of Youth Work. Obviously the aims and objectives that you have will affect the group and your activities.

Putting together a programme is hard work. The youth group that I used to run would meet two nights a week. On Friday night we would have a social event and on Sunday night we would have the spiritual programme. Trying to have an exciting programme for teenagers with high expectations, meeting together for almost a hundred evenings a year, tests energy and imagination to the limit. Of course, on top of the routine weekly events there were also weekends away, houseparties and Greenbelt, etc., etc.

Planning a programme is rather like a balancing act – too much of one thing or too little of another and the whole thing can fall apart. Your experience may be different, but I used to find that it was difficult to sustain a particular theme or Bible-study for more than three weeks. In response to the teenagers' cry for more teaching and the opportunity to learn more of what it means to be a Christian, we decided to put on a discussion series based on one of the Epistles. The teenagers said this was just what they wanted – the chance to get really stuck into some solid theological issues. Well, by week three they had had enough! They were bored and wanted to move on to something else. So the series was cut short and we decided to continue it periodically over a longer period of time so that the programme was not too heavy. Your teenagers perhaps are different but programme planning is not just about good ideas; it is also about being sensitive to the group and knowing its expectations, needs and demands. Well, anyway, how do you get the balance right?

POINTERS TO CONSIDER

Reason − Why do you meet?

If a meeting becomes a meeting for its own sake, then it usually will end up like a wet rag and be boring! What is the reason behind the meeting you have planned as part of your programme? Is it fellowship, or to have fun, prayer, teaching, outreach or worship? Of course, in any one evening a number of aims will be achieved, and as you look over your monthly or termly programme it should express a variety of reasons for meeting.

Here it is also important to balance the big successful events with the simple standard evenings. As part of our programme we would have coffee nights in members' homes and club nights that involved snooker, table-tennis, darts, games and the coffee bar/tuck shop. These were our simple standard social Friday nights. The teenagers would continually complain that they were not exciting enough, but the reason we had these social events regularly was because you could not sustain having something wildly exciting every week. There were also other reasons, like use of time, location and money. The interesting thing was that despite the complaints, almost all the teenagers used to turn up or drop in at some stage of the evening.

It is also important to balance out the successful events, those that you know everyone will enjoy and regard as a highlight. They are very useful in keeping the momentum of the group going. What are the successful events that you have staged? If you want some more ideas for evenings, look at the booklist at the end of this chapter. But, whatever the reason for your meeting, make sure you have got balance and variety.

Reflection – Who will meet?

What are the needs of the teenagers who will come along? The needs that they recognise for themselves may be different from the needs that you feel they have. Here mutual understanding and compromise is important. Mind you, not everyone in the group will have the same needs and interests. Things to reflect on are: How old are members of the group? What is their knowledge of the Bible? How well integrated are they with the life of the church? How much money do they have? What do they enjoy doing?

Resources – What is available?

Take a look at chapter 5, on Teaching. What gifts and skills do people in your group have? How are you allowing the programme of events to develop and express the skills of the leaders and young people? What about drama, dance, art work, speaking, leading discussion, and organisational and administrative skills? Think about your human resources, but also your technical ones as well. What do you have, and what can you get hold of – video equipment, projector, sound strips, literature, money, films?

If you properly assess your human and technical resources, you should be able to employ a great deal of variety in your programme. Since people learn in different ways, balance and variety are important. So use all available resources for your talks, quizzes, games, Bible study, discussion groups, simulation games, etc., etc.

News-sheet

With my youth group we used to publish a two-monthly programme. We found that with a three-monthly programme the organisational momentum would often tend to fall off during the last month. So we felt that two months was the better length of time. Your experience may be different. Do you publish a news-sheet or programme about what is happening? Some groups prefer not to because they would rather that their young people do not know what is happening. They prefer the element of surprise, and also emphasise the commitment to the group which involves coming regularly, irrespective of what is happening. This approach does have its value, but it is not the approach the majority of leaders and groups like to adopt. They want to know what is going to happen.

Do you print a news-sheet? If you do, go and get it out and have a look at it. What does it look like? I get a lot of youth group programmes sent to me. The best ones look interesting and colourful as soon as you see them. If you have an initial favourable reaction you think, 'This looks good. It is interesting! I think I would like to be involved with this.' Some of the best programmes I receive use different colours, are well designed and have contributions from the group members. You must have members of your group who are good at art work – get them to design something exciting. Also, there are now plenty of art books around that you can use to brighten up your programme. There are, moreover, plenty of pieces of artwork that you can use from magazines and papers. Photocopying your programmes for distribution is not very expensive and a good photocopier is very versatile.

The advantage of an attractive programme is that the young people know what is happening and where it is taking place. It is also a very useful item to give new members. It makes them feel welcome and informs them of what is going on, so they are probably more likely to turn up again.

Be ambitious

Be ambitious about what you do. As a rule, the crazier the idea the more successful it will be. You can usually judge how successful it has been by how much they moan about it afterwards. You can be ambitious in small things as well as more extravagant ones. One year with my youth group I said to them, 'Hey, if I organise a ski-ing trip who would like to come?' Well, the response was incredible, and twenty-four came with me. The idea at first seemed crazy and the responsibility frightening, but it worked.

Be ambitious, also, about whom you invite. If you write and ask someone, all he or she can do is say no.

SUGGESTIONS FOR FURTHER READING AND GROUP RESOURCES

Here are some of the common books of ideas for your youth group programme. But before you use any material, give yourself time to look through and familiarize yourself with it. It is often best to adapt even the most successful ideas or material so that it suits your group. Also, find out what material is available from your own denomination.

Nick Aiken, *Prayers for Teenagers* (Marshall Pickering).
Nick Aiken, *More Prayers for Teenagers* (Marshall Pickering).
Nick Aiken and Patrick Angier, *Youthbuilders* (Marshall Pickering).
—, *Big Ideas for Small Youth Groups* (Marshall Pickering).
Patrick Angier, *Junior Youthbuilders* (Marshall Pickering).
L. Coleman and D. Rydbury, *Serendipity Youth Bible*, series (Scripture Union)
Chris Herbert, *Alive to God* (Collins).
Bob Moffett, *Crowdbreakers* (Marshall Pickering).
—, *Crowdmakers* (Marshall Pickering).
—, *Power Pack* No. 1 and 2 (Scripture Union).
Phil Moon, *Young People and the Bible* (Marshall Pickering).
W. Rice, *Great Ideas for Small Groups* (Marshall Pickering).
W. Rice and Yaconelli, *Play It* (Marshall Pickering).
Emlyn Williams, *Consequences* (Scripture Union).
Pip Wilson, *Spectacular Stinking Rolling Magazine Book* (Marshall Pickering).
C.Y.F.A. *Syllabus* and *Teaching Manual* (Church Youth Fellowship Association – see Appendix of National Addresses).

22
PROGRAMME IDEAS

The books listed at the end of the previous chapter should be very useful in providing ideas for your group, likewise chapter 5 on Teaching. However, I thought I would group together a few particular ideas as a separate chapter. Some of them you may have tried, some you may not – but they may spark off a few thoughts.

One-night stand

This could take the form of an all-night visit to local centres where people are working; for example, a police station, hospital casualty department, fire station, chemical plant or post office. Apart from these obvious centres of all-night work, you may have local places of interest which are open twenty-four hours a day. Obviously, you will need prior liaison with the appropriate agencies.

You could start at 10.00 pm and arrange to finish at 6.00 am, with breakfast in the church hall. The event can be very educational and particularly memorable.

Bible-character role play

The activity needs careful handling and preparation, but it can be very worthwhile. You choose a passage from the Old or New Testament, then select people, or ask for volunteers, to take on the particular characters involved in the narrative. The individuals re-enact the passage, and then the group is encouraged to ask the characters what they felt. The individuals who played the parts are asked to stay in character and explore what might have been the feelings and attitudes that the real people originally felt.

You may, of course, give out a variety of passages and get everyone involved, so that each person has a character to play. The benefits are that it can often encourage good discussion and promote valuable personal insights.

Beach-party barbecue

Very few places in Britain are far from the sea. Even if you are up to two hours away, this is probably still worth doing on a good summer night. Acquire a minibus, barbecue facilities, sports equipment and music – and go for it! It can be a great time out. By the way, check up on a good beach site beforehand.

Car-treasure hunt

This needs to be well organised, but that is not too much trouble. You need someone to draw up a route and identify good clues, and then to type up and photocopy the clues involved. Club leaders' and parents' cars can be used. In fact, you may even want to involve members of the congregation and make it a church event. When all the cars have returned, after an hour or more, the sheets are marked, the time recorded and the results announced – with a suitable prize of course. If the use of cars is not feasible, simply do the hunting on foot.

One-prop parables

Form small groups of 3 to 5 people. Each group is given a prop – preferably an everyday item that can be used in a variety of ways. Then you give each group a parable to be acted out, using the prop as much as possible. Each group acts out its parable in turn to the others.

This can be excellent fun, and a useful opportunity for discussion. It also stretches people's imaginations and helps to promote insight into the passage. An alternative is to give the groups the *same* parable but different props, and see what happens.

Parents entertainment evening

This can be very worthwhile as an annual event. A personal

invitation to the parents is likely to result in a very high response. The occasion obviously needs careful preparation, requiring team work between leaders and teenagers. Your aim should be to involve all the young people in such things as drama, dance, singing, readings, catering and serving coffee. The actual entertainment for the parents need last as little as half an hour. You may also wish to have some form of exhibition of what the group has been doing over the past year.

The most positive side of the event is that it displays the encouraging side of the group and also provides an opportunity for the parents to identify with the group. It may also be an opportunity for you to meet the parents, particularly if they do not go to church.

Running supper

If you have not tried a running supper, then it is about time you did! The idea is very simple. You choose three or four homes where each course of the supper is served. In other words, one home for the starters, another for the main course, another for the pudding, and another for the coffee. Choose homes at a reasonable distance apart so that the whole movable feast is within a walking distance of 10–15 minutes. The food can either be prepared by group members or some 'tame' parents. The cost usually is fairly minimal.

Night hike

Start off at around 10.00 pm at the church hall and walk on a prearranged route until the early hours of the morning. It is important, of course, that you take care in choosing a safe route and that everyone is properly equipped, especially in coping with the delights of British weather. You may want to finish at about 2.00 am or walk through the night. If you return earlier you can camp in the church hall. But either way it is a good idea to meet together for breakfast. You may even wish to go into the early morning 8.00 am service if you hold the hike on a Saturday night.

Lock-in all-night vigil

You can do this over a twenty-four or twelve-hour period. It is best to use the church because it's a more interesting location and it gives more scope for expression. During the time you can do a variety of things: reading out of one of the books of the Bible, prayer groups, drama, meditations, talks, music, videos. In fact, you can add in whatever you choose. Such occasions, as you may imagine, create a strong sense of fellowship and identification with the group and the location that is used.

Auction supper for charity

Everyone comes with food to the meeting. It is wise to give the teenagers an idea of what you want them to bring. When everyone has arrived the food is auctioned to individuals. They can then, if they wish, team up with someone who has purchased another dish and share their food together. The proceeds are then given to charity. If you can get someone who is a bit of an extrovert to do the auction, then it will help the event to go with a bit of a sparkle.

Favourite Bible passages

Each member of the group is asked to prepare a short Bible passage which is special to them. On the night they are asked to read out the passage and explain what it means. Then they are asked why it is special to them. Finally, the rest of the group may be allowed to make comments about what they feel about the passage.

This encourages people to think and explore a Bible passage. It helps to foster a personal understanding of the text and how it applies to them. It can also give your teenagers confidence in speaking in public in what, it is hoped, will be a non-threatening atmosphere. However, if you do have some folk who are shy you can put people in pairs. A little bit of preparation is needed, and you really do not want too many passages. But it does not matter if you have a reading which comes up more than once, because people will have different perspectives on the text.

Agony Aunt evening

Collect over a period of weeks a selection of problems posed in the Agony Aunt columns of various magazines and papers. At the youth group meeting you may wish to form a panel or discuss in turn with the group what advice they would give to the person. When you have found out what advice they would offer, read out the comments by the Agony Aunt. Some answers from the young people will be serious, some stupid, but if you play it carefully you should be able to create a balance between humour and allowing personal insights into problems.

Multi-cultural evening

Select a country or culture which you want to look at. Let's say China, since that is easy. Encourage everyone to come dressed in the style of that country. Delegate members of the group to buy and cook some Chinese food or arrange something with the local Chinese take-away. You may wish to have a guest speaker who knows something about the country or, better still, a native of that land. Ask the relevant embassy for posters and information. Also music which is traditional to that country can be played, and if you have a film-strip or video as well, it can all add up to an enjoyable and informative evening.

Youth service

Most of you have probably done a youth service. If you have not done one recently, well, it's probably about time you did so. Youth services are very hard work and can be extremely good. I reluctantly began a youth service once a month at our daughter church, and it was not long before 200–300 people were turning up. There was, in fact, a wide range of ages. People came for the informality and spontaneity as well as for structure and order. If you let the young people organise it under careful oversight, what is produced through the music, prayers, dance, drama, meditation can be a beautiful act of worship. Be as imaginative and as adventurous as possible without offending the members of the congregation. Change the seating arrangements of the church, if that helps. Use banners and coloured lights, have interviews, use slides and pictures to illustrate the theme for the service. As long as you properly think through what you want to do and why you are doing it, it's amazing how creative a group of young people can be.

Face painting

This sounds a crazy idea – and it is. Everyone has to bring along water-based paint, mirrors, make-up, tissues and cleansing cream. All contributions are put on a central table and everyone pairs off. Then, in turn, they have the opportunity to paint their partner's face. You may want to give them some ideas – as, for example, a clown or an Indian, or a spider's web or anything. Of course, leaders have to join in. Since male make-up is now becoming popular, the boys don't mind getting involved. The results at the end of the evening should be recorded for posterity, so do have a camera ready. The evening can get everyone to relax and the physical contact is positive.

Silly-games night

Our next chapter is about Icebreakers, but don't overlook the fact that you can devote an entire evening to silly games. The benefits are obvious. All you need are about six good games to get everyone involved.

Question Time

This can be handled in a number of ways. You may stage it so that you have a panel which is either entirely made up of adults or else is a mixture of adults and young people. Prepared questions can be taken from the floor or gathered together beforehand and read out by the chairperson. You may wish to cover a range of topics or specialise in one subject for the evening such as parents, relationships, school, etc. To give it a more professional finish you may wish to use a microphone. If you attempt this a question box needs to be available for about a month beforehand, and it needs strong publicity every week. If you do not get a wide enough range of issues you may have to add in a few questions yourself.

Coffee party

A suitable home with very sympathetic parents can be a good venue for a coffee party. All that is needed is an ample supply of coffee, biscuits and background music. You may wish to present it as an opportunity to bring a friend along, and you could buy invitation cards for the young people to give to their friends. The advantage of such an occasion is that it requires minimal organisation and is a tremendously valuable opportunity for talking freely to the teenagers.

The Gulag Gospel

This simple activity helps the young people to understand something about the circumstances of those Christians who are persecuted for their faith, and also helps you to discover how much of the Bible they know.

When the group gathers together, confiscate all Bibles. Then give out a piece of paper and a pen, and divide the group into pairs. Ask them to write down from memory one of the Gospel stories. Give them about fifteen minutes to do this. After they have completed the story as accurately as they can, gather the group together. Ask each pair to read out what they have written and then get the group to arrange the stories in chronological order. This activity is a real test of memory and knowledge.

At the end of the evening it is worth highlighting the situation of Christians who are persecuted, particularly if you can refer to an individual. For information you will find it very helpful to contact Amnesty International (the address is listed at the end of ch. 6, page 44 above). Amnesty, in fact, have a Church section in their regular magazine which reports on those Christians who are in prison for their faith.

Christmas lights excursion

Most major cities do a reasonably good Christmas lighting display. So why not take the opportunity of hiring a minibus or coach and take the group to see the lights? A stop-off at a hamburger joint on the way home is obligatory. The event is simple and can be good fun.

Remember – whatever ideas you pick up, adapt them for your group. It works better that way.

23
ICE-BREAKERS

What is the point of using 'ice-breakers' in a group? Simply to break the ice and add a sense of fun and warmth to the atmosphere. But what do ice-breakers achieve?

- People relate to each other
- They relax
- They meet each other
- It helps to break down cliques
- They have fun

Since the atmosphere of a group is so important, ice-breakers have a valuable contribution to make. If the atmosphere expresses the feeling that the group is lively and enjoyable, then it will be the 'place to be'. Ice-breakers are useful when starting a new group or a new term. They are useful if you want to create a warm and relaxed atmosphere which will help foster discussion groups. They can be useful on a house-party or weekend away and when you have an influx of new members. They are also helpful when you want to lighten the atmosphere if an evening is getting too intense.

However, it is also important to use any activity sensitively. Some ice-breakers may not be appropriate for your group. Maybe they are too rowdy or too physical. Take care, because some games may be off-putting to a number of teenagers. Also, if you use too many games too often, the teenagers will get bored and regard the meeting as rather juvenile and trivial.

Anyway, here are some ice-breakers and games you may wish to use.

People Pyramid (version 1)

For this game you need five volunteers. The simple version involves asking the five to hold on to each other but to touch the floor with only four feet. No other part of the body is allowed to touch the ground. When the five have achieved this they must hold their position for fifteen seconds.

People Pyramid (version 2)

The second version is more difficult. Your five volunteers must only be touching the ground with two hands and two feet. Again, they must hold their position for fifteen seconds.

If you have got a large group you may want to have various teams of five competing against each other.

Dominoes

This game is very simple and does not involve physical contact. You line up everyone so that they stand behind each other, all facing in the same direction. The idea is that the person at the front of the line goes down into the squat position. As soon as he touches the ground, the person behind does the same, and the others follow in sequence. When the last person has squatted down, you reverse the process till everyone is standing up. You can do this simple activity a number of times until it is a smooth sequence and very fast.

Birdie on the Perch

If you have got a mixed group of roughly equal numbers, then this is a good activity game to play. Firstly, pair off everyone with a partner. Then get the girls to stand in a circle with their partners standing opposite them in an outer circle. The girls should then move around in an anti-clockwise direction while the boys move clockwise. As soon as you shout '*Birdie*' everyone must immediately find their partners, with the boys going down on one knee and the girls sitting on their extended knee. You may wish to have a couple of practice attempts. When you begin properly you simply eliminate the last pair to get into position. Eventually you end up with a winning couple. The game is great fun.

Body Movement

With this activity, which only really works with a group of more than seventeen, you again ask everyone to choose a partner. Having done so, you tell them to stand in two straight lines beside each other. You then require them to lie on their backs on the floor, head to head with their partner and shoulder to shoulder with the person beside them. You ask them to put their arms in the air. Onto the raised hands you lower the odd person who is left over, requiring him or her to lie flat facing the ceiling. You then move this upheld body along the line of the hands. This game usually causes great amusement, and if you have a small group you can get each couple at the front to get up and go to the end so you have got a continuous movement of the person till the end of the room. And then? Well, bring them back again!

Bumpy Ride

This game is similar to the above except that it is slightly more civilised. Get everyone to lie on the floor on their backs beside each other, alternately lying head to foot. Put a mattress on top of the front of the line and ask someone to lie on it and then pass him or her and the mattress along the line, and back again. If you have got a large group you could have two teams, or you can do it as a relay. Get the boys to lie on the floor and convey the girls in turn on the mattress from one end of the room to the other.

All in a Knot

This game can be played with any number more than seven and fewer than twenty-four. Get everyone to stand in a circle shoulder to shoulder. They put out their hands in front of them and wave them all around, seeking to grab another person's hand with their left hand and then with their right. For this activity to work they must only hold two hands in total, one with their right and one with their left. You then ask them to unravel so that they are standing in a circle holding hands. This will involve all sorts of contortions but it can be done if people have followed instructions.

Did You Know?

Supply your group with pen and paper. Ask them to write down six relatively unknown facts about themselves, such as a place they have visited, their favourite colour, TV personality, car, breakfast cereal, sport, etc. Give them about ten minutes to put down all six. Make sure they do not put their names on the paper. Ask them to fold up the papers and place them in a container. Then ask someone to pick out one piece of paper and slowly read out the six facts. At each stage everyone tries to guess who the person is. This ice-breaker works well with older teenagers.

Find the person with . . .

Here are two very good games to mix everyone up and break down barriers. Reproduce the two lists below and hand out pencils or pens and sheets of paper to everybody. Tell them to assign a person's name to each item. When someone has filled in all the items get everyone to sit down, and read out the results and see who agrees or disagrees with the findings.

List 1: Find the person with the

1 deepest voice
2 longest eyelashes
3 dishiest smile
4 shortest hair
5 reddest lips
6 dirtiest shoes
7 fiercest frown
8 most kissable face
9 hairiest hand
10 most beautiful hair
11 knobbliest knees
12 blondest curls
13 firmest handshake
14 shyest look
15 longest nails
16 biggest feet
17 bluest eyes
18 cheekiest grin
19 warmest cuddle
20 most intellectual look
21 the most colourful
   wristwatch

22 most money
23 farthest to go home
24 biggest appetite

25 smoothest chin
26 bushiest eyebrows

List 2: Find the person

1 born furthest away
2 with most brothers and/or sisters
3 with most unusual pet
4 with strangest fear
5 with weirdest allergy
6 with most interesing ambition
7 who has most awful nightmares
8 who has oddest history
9 who has most eccentric relative
10 who speaks the most languages
11 who has had most embarrassing true incident

12 who has had funniest true incident happen to them
13 who has had most uncanny experience
14 who is best read
15 who is most independent
16 who has oddest family custom
17 who got into worst trouble at school
18 who has had most dramatic true life experience

Back to Back

Gather people into pairs standing back to back. Then get them to sit down, leaning against each other but without using their hands. That's easy – but then get them to stand up. Not so easy! After they have tried that a few times, gather them into a group of four, with backs leaning against each other in a square. Then get them to sit down and stand up! This game should produce a few laughs.

Are You Sitting Comfortably?

The whole group should stand in a circle, all facing in a clockwise direction. Each should be almost touching the person in front. Then, given the word, each one should simultaneously sit gently on the lap of the person behind them. If that proves too easy, see how long the group can stay seated in the circle; or better still see if you can get the group to walk collectively while seated on each other's lap.

Killer Wink

Everybody, except one individual, should sit on the floor in a circle. The individual is then asked to leave the room while a 'killer' is chosen. Then the individual comes back into the room and is asked to stand in the centre of the circle. He or she is asked to guess who the 'killer' is. Meanwhile the person chosen as the killer murders someone by winking. The murdered individual should fall over and die. The game goes on until the individual has guessed who the killer is.

Snowball Showdown

The group is divided into two teams, each of which is supplied with a pile of old newspapers. The two teams are arranged in a straight line facing each other about seven feet apart. On the word 'go' everyone has to make as many paper snowballs as they can and throw them at the opposition. The winner is the team which has flung the most paper snowballs on the opposition side. This game is best with a time limit of, say, 3–4 minutes. It usually dissolves into chaos but it is great fun!

Road Atlas

Give each individual a large piece of paper and a coloured pen, with the instruction to put a mark on the bottom left-hand corner which represents the day he or she was born, and a mark on the top right-hand corner which represents the present day. All participants are then asked to draw a map of their life, beginning at birth, pictorially indicating any significant events along the way – for example, a stay in hospital, their first school, places they have visited, things they have done. When all have finished, pair each off with someone they least know in the group and then get them to explain to each other what they have drawn.

I Think . . .

Give each individual a pen and a large sheet of paper. Ask everyone to draw a line which divides the paper in half, then into quarters. Having done that ask them to draw in each quarter something they have been thinking about and that has been uppermost in their thoughts over the past week. When they have done their drawing, either divide them into pairs or into fours to explain their pictures, or let each person share what he has drawn with the whole group.

Follow the Leader

This game is very like 'Killer Wink'. Everyone sits in a circle and a leader is chosen from the group while someone else is sent out of the room. Upon this latter's return, he or she is placed in the centre of the group. The group members should then follow the actions of the chosen leader – for example, scratching heads, crossing legs, etc. The person in the centre has, of course, to guess who the leader is. When caught, the leader becomes the person in the centre, and a new leader is appointed.

Trust Me

This is a great ice-breaker to lead into a discussion or Bible study on faith. Pair everyone off, and blindfold one person in each pair. The couples then go all around the building for about five minutes, the 'sighted' leading the 'blind'. When they come back use the exercise as an opportunity to discuss what the blindfolded partners felt – their trust in the one who was guiding them, their sense of fear and insecurity. See what theological lessons you can draw out of what is said.

Paper Skyscraper

Divide the group into teams with an equal amount of newspaper, and supply them with Sellotape. With a time limit of five minutes, ask them to construct a paper skyscraper. The winning team will be the group which manages to construct the highest tower without its falling over.

Tickle Factor

The group should stand in a circle, with everybody facing clockwise. Each one should put hands on the waist of the person in front, and tickle. Once the circle has broken up – in other words, after about three seconds – bring everyone back and get them to face the anti-clockwise direction and do the same. You cannot help but be amused by this ice-breaker.

Who Am I?

Each person, on arrival, has the name of a famous individual pinned on to his or her back. All have then to find out who they are by asking questions of everybody else. The replies must only be either 'yes' or 'no'. When the person guesses correctly, he or she is out of the game.

On the Ball

This is a good activity to help everyone know and memorise everyone else's name. The group should stand in a circle. The leader says his or her name and then throws a ball to a person and announces that person's name. The latter, on catching the ball, repeats his name and gives out the name of the person to whom the ball is next going to be thrown. After a few minutes everyone should have caught the ball and thrown it to someone else. By varying the pace you can keep the game going for some time. The effect is that, after about five minutes, everyone should be aware of everyone else's name.

Rip Off

Everyone is given a large piece of newspaper. The lights are then turned off and all have to tear their piece of paper into as long a strip as possible. There should be a time limit of 4 or 5 minutes. The person with the longest strip is the winner.

I Don't Believe You

This game is good for a group who know each other fairly well. Give everybody a pen and a piece of paper. On it they should write three true and one untrue thing about themselves.

Then, in turn, each person has to guess which statement is untrue, as it is read out by each individual in turn. Those who spot the untrue statement can award themselves a point. The person at the end with the highest number of points is the winner.

Orange Peel

A golden oldie which is always fun. Form a line, or two if you have got a large group. The person at the front is given an orange to be held between chin and chest. This orange then has to be passed to each person along the line, and it must be conveyed between the chin and the chest. If the orange is dropped, it goes back to the beginning of the line and the race begins again.

Measuring Up

Line everyone up at random, standing them on chairs. They then have to arrange themselves in order of ascending height from the left-hand side. They are not allowed to step down from the line of chairs and must take care to hold on to each other as they pass along measuring their height in comparison with each other. The game involves physical contact; if it proves to be too simple, reverse the process and ask them all to change around and ascend in height from the right-hand side.

SUGGESTIONS FOR FURTHER READING

In the list given at the end of chapter 21 (page 153 above), there are five which are particularly good in providing ideas for ice-breakers: Dearling and Armstrong, *The Youth Games Book*; Moffett, *Crowdbreakers*; and Rice and Yaconelli, *Play It*; Aiken, *Big Ideas for Small Youth Groups*; Aiken and Angier, *Youthbuilders*. These could keep you going for years!

24
MUSIC AND WORSHIP*

Music is a very powerful medium which evokes various feelings and emotions. Even an image on a TV screen can be made frightening or hilarious by the music soundtrack. Music is around and in us. Your pulse is beating out the rhythm of your heart as you read.

Our youngest child, while only ten months old, responds to music with a sway, a smile and a clap. However, when a melancholy track from an album is played, his response is more likely to be a stare and a rigid stance, as though listening to the music through his hands.

Most young people take their music seriously; it matters to them. They listen to it and are even united and divided by it in tribal fashion. Of course, fashion plays a huge part in their choice of music. Their music is their style, and style is part of what makes them tick. Many teenagers play music like flying a flag that says, 'Hey, this is me!' or 'This is what I want to say.' Their musical tastes will, of course, develop and their allegiances will be short-lived, changing with the style that media and friends dictate.

Young people generally can hear the words to their pop songs! And the teenage music magazines print out the lyrics of all the top chart songs. Songs of the nineties are different in styles and contents from those of the eighties. Lyrics of the eighties have less of the mindless sexism of the seventies. The eighties have also brought us the records for charity. Young people have responded to the call of their

*This chapter is contributed by Mike King.

171

pop heroes to feed the world, or support a children's hospital.

Music is a gift from God and we should use it. In God's Church, music can be used for worship, praise, encouragement and inspiration. Teenagers have a capacity to keep singing beyond the church service into the young people's group meeting. Through singing they memorise the words. Paul the Apostle said 'Faith comes by hearing.' Therefore, if our young people have a capacity to hear and retrieve God-centred lyrics that reveal the character of Jesus, then we as leaders should use the music potential to the full.

WORSHIP

Before we consider practical hints for youth leaders, it is essential we remember we are called to love God and worship him. The Bible's word for worship means 'to bow down', 'to draw near to and adore'. Worship is a response of intimacy to God along with the giving of ourselves, talents, resources and money (Romans 12:1). The outcome of this is of great value! (Romans 12:2).

What is Christian Worship?

1 *To God and for God*. Worship pleases God. We express confession, thanks and adoration to:

The Father: Jesus said, 'You shall worship the Lord your God and Him only shall you serve' (Matthew 4:10b).

The Son: As God, Jesus is to be worshipped. He deserves worship (John 20:28; Luke 24:52) and He is worshipped in heaven (Revelation 5:8–13) with His Father.

2 *Intimacy with God*. In worship we are expressing our real selves to Him, we belong to him and are freely giving love to God (Psalm 18:11). An expression of Wow! God you are amazing, awesome, A1! We submit to Him, respect and honour Him (Psalm 95:1, 2 & Psalm 96:1–3).

3 *From God to us.* As we worship our Father God, raise Him high and honour Him, He draws us into His presence. He communicates to us through gifts of His spirit: preaching, teaching, prophecy, encouragement and more, converting, renewing, equipping, strengthening, healing and challenging.

What on earth makes us think we can sing to God? Why should He accept our praise and worship? Answer – because of what Jesus did on the Cross. In Hebrews (10:10, 19) we discover we have been made holy by His offering. We can have full confidence to enter into God's presence because of Jesus. Just imagine the 82-foot curtain in the great Jewish temple. It hung there to separate people from the place called the Holy of Holies. That massive tapestry was ripped apart when Jesus died. God has shown us that the way to Him is open through Jesus.

When Jesus spoke to the outcast woman at the well (John 4), He said: God is looking for worshippers who will worship in Spirit and in truth (reality).

In Spirit – worship that isn't inspired by God but only by human nature may be sincere, but that's not enough. The Holy Spirit creates in us a desire to adore God. Our confidence must be in the Spirit (Philippians 3:3). The Holy Spirit helps us express our love to God (Romans 8:26). Through Jesus we are able to approach the Father and it is the Holy Spirit who comes to give us access into the presence of the Father (Ephesians 2:18).

In Truth – the head may be bowed, and the arm raised, but God wants the decision-making part of us to bow in true adoration.

Ways to express worship

Scripture shows us we can worship God with:

- our minds and understanding: singing, praying, silence.
- our spirits: tongues (1 Corinthians 14).
- our bodies: playing instruments, kneeling, dancing, bowing, lifting hands (Exodus 4:31; Nehemiah 8:6).

Our singing and praying can vary. We can use Scripture and Liturgy (established formulas for public worship). In Acts, the first Christians raised their voice together in praise and prayer, combining Scripture and their own words as the Spirit led them (Acts 4:23–31). Paul used the earliest established Christian hymns (Ephesians 5:19).

WORDS AND MUSIC

Think about the words

Lyrics used for worship and praise need to reflect the inner change in us, that has an outworking in action. Our singing is a response to the Christ who is alive today! The lyrics need to reflect the reality of our faith and our desire. Sometimes they are the first steps of a faltering seeker. We sing to acknowledge and corporately proclaim who God is, and thank Him for what He has done and is doing. The Psalms express human weakness, failings, sadness and desperation, as well as joy and triumph. Our singing can be used to express repentance, thanks, expectancy – to tell a story and bring needs to the surface.

Understand the aim of the lyrics

When choosing songs for a church gathering or a young people's evening, our choice of material needs to take into account the direction of the lyrics. For interest, scan the lyrics in a hymn book and a newer song book. Many of the older songs are about God and about the Christian life, while many of the newer ones tend to be expressions to God. Some lyrics are words we can sing to encourage one another to worship, saying 'Come let's worship the King together', or an exhortation to 'open our eyes and see His glory'. These are particularly helpful at the beginning of a time of praise.

Those of us who are leading praise and worship need sensitivity to the lyrics, choosing songs that will flow into a time of confession, of thankgiving and of adoration.

Styles of music

As leaders in churches we need integrity, openness and vision. Music is both a dividing and a uniting factor, as already mentioned.

One problem is that many young people would happily sing loud and extrovert songs like 'Be bold, Hosanna, and Rejoice' all evening! We, however, know that our celebration of God should also involve the quiet, thoughtful, meditative songs as well. How often I have noticed young people deeply touched by the gentler songs, such as 'What kind of love is this?' or 'Let the Son of God enfold you!' The other side of the coin is that teenagers can see through a dull response from a congregation reciting from the ASB without emotion 'let your people shout for joy'. They can tell if there isn't joy.

Our faith is based in historical fact. God's church is based in history and has a heritage. Songs from the past, great hymns like 'Thine be the glory', blend with the thousands of new songs written in the last decade. How often we are exhorted in Scripture to sing to the Lord a new song (Psalm 33:3, 96:1; Isaiah 42:10).

Words and music and young people

Paul the Apostle said, 'In the church I would rather speak five intelligible words to instruct others than ten thousand words in a tongue!' (1 Corinthians 14:19). Jesus spoke the street language of his day. This makes us realise that the words we use in our worship need to be accessible and relevant to young minds, and not lyrics held in a time warp or the language of Elizabethan England. Young people must be allowed to express their faith, and what they would want to say to God, through a vehicle they can relate to. To do otherwise would mean we older ones are foisting another barrier on to teenagers adoring and enjoying God's presence in worship today.

Our particular taste in music should be flexible so that, in being rooted in unity, we can collectively taste and see that the Lord is good. Our various and multi-coloured styles of music like a spectrum come together as one light of adoration back to God.

PRACTICAL HINTS AND ADVICE

The leader's goal

By leading and playing we are helping people to worship, encouraging others to join us (this is best done not by 'prodding' but by leaders themselves worshipping). Our job is to escort people into God's presence, a closeness with Him, and with one another. What about nerves and unhelpful feelings in leading? Sometimes when we are down or hassled, nervous about playing or feeling awkward, we need to remember God helps us through these situations. He honours trust and our 'sticking in there' to serve Him. Jesus spoke of 'meeting together in agreement' (Matthew 18:19, 20). The word for meet means 'led together', so we need to sense God's leading in our task (and not just turning up 'cos it's wot I usually do'!).

Many do not come to worship prepared – often including us! When the job is hard we need to remember our task is to offer 'a sacrifice of praise' so that cold hearts can be touched and warmed by God.

New song material

These are some of the books containing newer songs, available from most Christian book shops:
Mission Praise, Junior Praise and *Carol Praise* (Marshall Pickering)
Spirit of Praise, Downs Songbooks (Word/New Frontiers)
*Combined Hymns and Songs of Fellowship (Kingsway Publications)

Using an overhead projector

Many congregations and young people's groups are realising the benefit of songs shown on a large screen by an overhead

---

*The music in these books is available on tape. This is invaluable for the music groups learning songs.

projector. No shuffling of pages, or heads dug into hymn books! Teenagers I know find the OHP a great assistance in relaxing and concentrating on God in praise and worship.

Copyright

The Christian Music Association has been formed, and for an annual fee paid to it, a church is permitted to copy and photocopy songs and music. The fee depends on the size of the congregation or church group. Fuller details are available from Christian Copyright Licensing, Glyndley Manor, Stone Cross, Eastbourne, East Sussex BN24 5BS.

Making acetates

I have found the most professional method is to use a photocopier, enlarging from the song book, then enlarging that copy; again enlarge a third copy and position centrally on A4 paper. Then feed through photocopy acetate to make final print out.

Instruments to form a Music Group

The variety of instruments that can work together with any number of singers is, of course, endless. Here are a few ideas:

- a piano and guitar is an effective combination;
- guitars; e.g. one strumming, the other picking;
- guitar, piano, bass with flute or saxophone;
- the above with drums and/or synthesizer;
- piano, guitar, cello, violin, clarinet.

With all of these variations it is good to have a basic male and female lead vocal, and then any number of singers up to a choir.

Starting a Music Group

Be wary of young musicians! Choose, don't call for volunteers (the results can be heartbreaking). Start small, set a target — e.g. three or four songs at the young people's evening, etc. Give, or delegate, leadership: good groups don't just happen. Otherwise follow the practical rules listed at the end of this section.

Amplification

Volume is again a matter of taste. But in large rooms, halls or church buildings, amplification is very helpful. Requirements will vary. Here's a basic idea for a typical large room or hall.

For vocals: 100 watt amplifier, 2 speakers. A couple of microphones on stands can pick up a well positioned group of singers. (Beware of cheap microphones which feedback!)

Bass: 50 watt Combo (that is a combined amplifier and speaker in one box). Roland 'Cube' is good.

Keyboard: Roland also have a 'Cube' combo designed for synthesizers and electric pianos.

Guitar: 30 watt combo. Session amplifiers are good value, as well as Fender, Roland.

You will usually find local music dealers willing to give time and advice. Secondhand instruments can be purchased from the classified section of a music paper called *Melody Maker*.

Buying instruments

These days the choice of guitars, keyboards, acoustic and electronic drums is so wide that the best advice is try them out at your local dealer. Stiff competition has pushed quality up and prices down. One instrument I will mention as a good investment for a local church is the Roland D50 Keyboard. It costs around £1,200 but its versatility and sounds (which include piano and strings) make it a good buy. There is also a wide range of excellent Yamaha Keyboards.

Learning to be a good administrator

The leader of a music group needs to be a good team person. Liaising with those preaching, speaking or leading the service is essential. The Holy Spirit inspires prayerful planning before a service, as well as during the praise and worship. It is easier to change nearer the time, or in the time of worship, if you have prepared a plan beforehand. Preparing groups of two or three songs that flow together is helpful. These sections can then be moved easily without disruption to a nervous and book-laden group of musicians.

As the group matures it will become more adaptable. Where only one or two instruments are being used, changing the direction the songs are going in is that much easier. The music leader needs to be like Philip, prepared to take a different road as the Spirit leads! (Acts 8:26).

This is a sample of a layout that I prepare and photocopy for all musicians involved in a service. If I were leading with guitar only at the youth group this of course would not be required.

St George's 6.30 PRAISE
Theme: Light of the World John 8:12

Words	Music	Key	Song	Arrangement
Photo copy	New Songs 88 No. 24	A	Lord the Light of your Love	Intro: Synth Double chorus at end
Photo copy	Songs of Fellowship 457	D	O let the Son of God enfold you	Intro: piano/Synth last line of chorus

---

Arrangement tips

Work out which instruments are to do the introductions – for example piano, or guitar first or last two lines of verse.

Dynamics: More interest can be created by the group if instruments don't all play all the time. For example, have sections with just a piano or a guitar – hold back, leave space, build to a fuller sound. All these ideas need sensitivity and time spent working things out. Sometimes it is effective towards the end of a song to have a verse with vocals only, then full in for the chorus. Do watch your timing though! Also watch out for lead frills that get messy, especially if there are two keyboards and a guitar. Harmonies need to be well worked out, and are usually better if allowed to build towards the end of a song.

A music group must sound good as a whole; each person should listen to the others and not do their own thing.

Services with emphasis on young people

Services using contemporary worship, where teenagers are actively involved in readings, prayers, etc. can be constructive. The young people will ask their friends from school. Evangelism becomes more natural, they can say 'come and see'.

Music in youth and home groups

Singing in the group can break the barrier of teenage nerves. It gives young people a chance to say something or to pray the prayer they wouldn't have had the courage to, without the vehicle of song. Singing the words builds their faith together and assists a freer flow of their talents, conversation, sharing of their experience and gifts for the rest of the meeting.

Yes, there will be some who won't sing, who will hide behind books and mess around, but in love we need to persevere. When the songs are voiced meaningfully, God is pleased. The songs focus the teenagers' thoughts on Him. And as Christian youth work is about discipling, that is helpful.

Unchurched teenagers in the group

Singing in the youth group can be a first link in their uttering words of Christian truth. A sentence may click, a thought recalled later.

Music leader introductions to the congregation

Mention a line from the song, or perhaps a sentence of Scripture. Remind the worshippers of a promise of God, or a couple of sentences to escort their thoughts to God. Never prod or try to work them up, and worship your Father God yourself. Use songs that go one into another without introductions, and use silence.

Silence can be used after a song. Perhaps invite people at the start of a song to use the brief silence that will follow, to concentrate on God, or an attribute like His love, light, faithfulness. In between songs of thanks perhaps encourage the congregation to one-sentence open prayers of thanks. Providing there is a certain freedom allowed in your youth group or church service, be prepared to change direction in song choice. Be open to the Holy Spirit. 'Is this a moment for confession, adoration, thanks or silence?'

N.B. We are all learners, we make mistakes, and being open to change can make us feel very uncomfortable! But then our strength isn't *our* strength – the Lord is our strength.

Inviting worship leaders

Now and again invite guests to lead worship and to share their faith. This can enrich, and add experience to the life of a church. Share your church's talent!

Writing songs for worship and praise

Try to use words teenagers can understand. Sentences can be unpacked. For example, instead of 'Hallowed be your name', you could say, 'May Your name be honoured'. I try to impart 'power-words' like 'Justified', into a line like 'Justif-I'd never gone wrong'. Here we are dove-tailing in teaching and evangelism. It is our duty to unveil some of the Gospel language – great truths God would wish teenagers to know.

Those with writing and composing skills need channelling in a local church or youth group, so that they can develop and find expression for their gift.

Adapting songs with new words

This can be helpful for different situations. For example, to a song like 'Open Our Eyes' I've given an evangelistic slant, adapting as a prayer for others:

> So shine in our lives Lord, that we can show Jesus,
> Reach out and touch them, and show that we love them.
> Shine in our speech Lord and help us to listen
> Open their eyes Lord and glorify Jesus.

181

Using scripture

Carefully constructed sentences using Bible verses can make good songs. For example:

> For God so loved the world He gave His only Son
> That whoever trusts and relies in Him shall live.
> We all have gone astray each to his own way
> The Lord has laid on Him our guilt and wrong.

> Revealed in human flesh, fulness of God expressed
> He opened up the way into His peace
> God sent His righteous Son, raised high His Holy One
> The light still shines in the dark, and leads to life.

Other songs to communicate

There isn't space to discuss the many varied songs that can be written, the many themes and styles. Teenage bands need to have a direction, and an aim. 'Is this song for entertainment, are the lyrics for fun, are they a challenge, are they highlighting a need or a situation?'

If aiming to communicate, be aware that style of music can close doors as well as open them. One band I was in played a gig in a Brixton youth club. Soul or reggae would have been fine, but not our style – the result was a fiasco. Not until we put our instruments down, sat down and chatted about Jesus did they respond!

Here's part of a song written for teenagers, used in a Tear Fund filmstrip a few years ago:

> Just left school but there's no work around,
> Our hopes and plans have all gone wrong.
> Are politicians to blame, or all these foreign faces?
> Lord, it's so frustrating, agitating, aggravating,
> Waiting on the dole.

> Watching the TV news about refugees,
> The children of war without a home.
> Can I switch off, or just turn over –
> From all their fears, all their needs, so many tears?
> Lord, do I want to know?

Using bands for young people's events

Christian bands, duos and artistes are available for hire. Contact can be made through record companies like Word, Kingsway, Marshall Pickering, and Ears and Eyes and through Christian teenage press. Use local talent when you can, perhaps as a support act. Be aware of performers' aims. In other words, are they evangelistic or for entertainment only?

Organisers of evangelistic and celebration concerts need to: pray, plan, advertise, be aware of technical details, pray for and with musicians, provide hospitality and lads to lift gear, provide follow up to those challenged, make available Christians gifted in chatting to teenagers, and a welcoming place to chat.

Using recorded music A useful variation in a chat, and helpful for many reasons already mentioned, in youth group meetings and assemblies.

Christian records: larger Christian bookshops stock records from the labels mentioned above. Reggae, rock, soul, ballads to blasters. Try and find out what's available. Greenbelt festival is a useful show-case for some of the performance talent available. Other festivals and events highlight what's new in Christian worship and praise.

. . . and Secular! some of the emotions expressed in songs from the pop chart convey something we can use as a pointer to God's thoughts, and Christian values. In an assembly, for instance, part of a song can accentuate a theme we are trying to get over. We do need to be careful and creative! Here are some samples of lines I heard on fifteen minutes of morning radio:

'I am what I am, a family man.'
'Someone who'll take away the heartache, the loneliness, the pain.'
'You broke my heart, now I'm aching for you.'
'Promises, we forget all our promises.'

MUSIC AND WORSHIP

Alternative worship

In the past few years there has been a real growth in alternative style worship events. They have often captured the headlines in the church and secular press because of their radical and unorthodox approach to worship. Here in Guildford a group of youth leaders from various churches now hold an alternative worship experience at a local nightclub. It certainly has attracted the support of young people, with over 500 turning up every other month. But the experience in Guildford is just one among many around the country. The most well known is the 'Nine O'clock Service', in Sheffield.

In the main these alternative services have sought effectively to communicate with today's young people and to relate to their culture as a means to communicate the Christian faith. It is difficult to sum up all the component parts of an alternative worship event since the content and style do vary according to local emphasis.

However the point for you as a parish youth leader is that alternative worship events show that you can be very imaginative about what you use in worship. It may be using traditional symbols such as water and incense in a new and more culturally meaningful way. It may be using an entertaining and fast-moving programme which puts worship in the context of interviews, dance music, drama and multi-coloured lighting. The important common denominator to these events is that people have employed their imagination and sought to use more contemporary meaningful things to assist in worship. Providing it does not become a religious form of entertainment but actually helps people to worship God, then alternative worship events can be very helpful.

If you would like to think this through further then look at Pete Ward's book called *Worship and Youth Culture: a guide to making services radical and relevant*, published by Marshall Pickering.

TEN PRACTICAL RULES FOR A PRAISE/WORSHIP GROUP

1 *Share lives.* Get to know each other as friends. Have a meal, chat over a cup of tea, share ideas and problems as they arise.
2 *Learn.* Develop an understanding of what worship involves.
3 *Pray.* Make time for listening to God, make your requests for guidance etc.
4 *Support.* Help each other, encourage the leader and let him or her lead! Forgive mistakes and heated moments. Sharpen one another creatively (Proverbs 27:17) and listen to one another.
5 *Practice.* Work hard individually, and together. Keep clear notes on arrangements. Practice can be hard graft! Play to the best of your ability for God now, and improve.
6 *Prepare.* The Holy Spirit inspires both prayerful planning before a service and during.
7 *Grow in sensitivity.* Deploy songs for situations, gradually learning with confidence to change with the flow – e.g. praise, confession, etc.
8 *Time before worship/service.* Pray, practise, then relax. Try and meet with ministers and others involved in the service. Have a time of quiet. Be prayed for.
9 *Accept criticism.* Weigh it up. It *can* be very useful.
10 *Worship!* Have faith in God, be expectant.

'. . . Let's lift up high His name together' (Psalm 34:3).

25
DRAMA*

INTRODUCTION

A young man, gold ear-rings dangling from one ear, spikey hair carefully highlighted, moves across the room. A plumpish girl wearing spectacles and a puff-ball skirt, stands by a pillar in the room. He approaches her. Well, what will they say to each other? Will he ask her what night she's free? Would she like to go and see Dire Straits at Wembley? She looks up. She speaks to him, sadly: 'Sir, they have taken the body of my master away and I don't know where they have laid him.' He looks lovingly at her. 'Mary', he says in a soft and warm voice. 'Master?' – she hesitates. Yes, you know the rest.

Two young people, apparently conforming in so many ways to their age group, yet caught up in enacting the events of Easter morning. An attentive crowd watching them, waiting. Keen to present their own prepared drama.

The place – Grafham. Time – Saturday afternoon of a youth leaders' weekend. However, it could equally have been any youth club or group – any evening or weekend. Drama is probably the most portable of all the arts.

One person with a few words and a gesture or two can provide entertainment or teaching, or new insight – or all three. Add a few simple props, some basic costumes and you have a one man show. You may even have an audience!

Why drama?

From the earliest times, mankind has transmitted ideas,

*This chapter is contributed by Edward Bonner.

knowledge, comprehension through a number of different media. Speaking and representing, writing and reading, illustrating and imitating. Of these, the visual image has consistently emerged as the most effective and instantaneous method of reaching people. You've heard it said, 'One picture speaks a thousand words'. Ask yourself: How true is this of me? Before you answer, consider that there has never been an age more exposed to, and affected by, visual images.

HOW TO START

Most children like to have a go at 'acting'. At home this often takes the form of mimicking a well-known TV role. Charades are popular, too. As they come into their teens, the girls begin to absorb the romantic and feminine images from reading or television, and the boys struggle with early 'machoism'.

When you broadcast your intention to set up a Drama Group, or to have drama within the youth club, or just that 'we're doing a play this Easter' – then be sensitive towards the small and disguisedly nervous group who stay behind after the evening service, or meet in the kitchen towards the end of the normal youth evening. Many of them will be bursting with enthusiasm but almost certainly misinformed as to what is called for, or indeed needed. Let me offer some advice: start by organising a Drama Workshop for young people.

Starting with a Drama Workshop

Invite all those who turned up at the preliminary meeting. Pick the most suitable day and time when you think you can obtain the largest attendance. Agree with the keeper of the church hall or rooms, that it's all right to have chairs moved out of the way (remember to keep to the rule 'leave the place as you found it').

Now, advertise your workshop! You may want to invite some local drama teacher or director to run it for you (yes, I do take bookings). However, do ask the leader what he or she intends to do. Workshop groups must *do* things to be useful, not listen to an hour's lecture on 'plays I have produced' or 'audiences I have thrilled'.

A typical first workshop for a drama group might look like this:

1	Welcome	
2	Prayer	
3	Outline of the next few hours	
4	Physical exercise 1 – Movement	5 minutes
	2 – Co-ordination	
	Pair off for	
5	3 – Relating to each other	5 minutes
6	*Mental alertness*	
	Memory words	2 minutes
	Name exchange	3 minutes
	Form groups for	
7	First ad lib script – Hand out/Discuss	10 minutes
+	Comfort break	5 minutes
8	Group work	10 minutes
9	Ad lib presentation	20 minutes
+	Coffee break – Leader notes	15 minutes
10	2nd ad lib script ideas	10 minutes
11	Preparation	20 minutes
12	Presentation	20 minutes
+	Break	10 minutes
13	Reform in larger groups for 10–12 above (optional)	50 minutes
	Total time	*3 hours*

On the day, arrive early and clear the hall of all chairs, tables, etc., so as to leave sufficient space for twenty energetic bodies to move around in (about 40 square feet per person is reasonable). If you have smaller premises, you may have to do this exercise in two groups, with one group sitting it out alternately. This, of course, can be quite instructive in its own way.

Now, what is the purpose of such an event?

Firstly: it reminds everyone that drama is about physical and mental challenges, as much as emotional self-indulgence – so you have to be in condition in all sorts of ways.

Secondly: it stresses how much discipline those three elements demand, emotionally and mentally.

Thirdly: it demonstrates how much a task team drama really is.

Finally: it should dispense with any notion that drama is about learning a few lines and posturing as your favourite television character.

What should you expect at the end of the session? Well, you may find that, before three hours are over, some people have already had their eyes opened. They may decide that play acting is not for them, especially the hard work! Others will regard the experience as enough for a while.

However, some of your group will stick with you and it is important to understand what you will suggest they do next.

Taking the next steps

Let me give you a few options:

1 Take the initiative with all those who want to give it a go. Fix an evening when they want to meet. You will want to discuss on that first evening what you intend to perform. (Have a look at the section on Material, below.)

2 Ask for views from those who want to perform a full-length play, as distinct from having a drama interest within the group. If this body of opinion is greater, then you will have to decide to balance your approach to your organisation.

3 It could be that both are thought equally valid as aims of the group. Fine – but start simple and then keep the interest alive by planning a major event every so often.

4 Arrange to have another workshop after a period of time. Of course, whichever option you choose to follow, there are certain arrangements you must make.

Book a rehearsal place. No, not a friend's living room or the back of the double garage. Remember what you have just gone through in the workshop. It involves having space for movement and a staging area, however small. Drama can also be noisy from time to time, so you need to be on neutral ground.

Tell your clergy (and hall keeper) what you will be doing and which evening. If it is to be part of the youth evening, you should discuss it with other leaders and have them understand what you will be doing. Provided you have planned your sessions and know what you want to do with the group, your initiative should be welcome.

Communicate. Make sure all the people who wanted to join in are informed of time and place. It is helpful if you also ensure that they know what is going to be covered in the first few sessions. Especially useful is a handout advising that there will be physical activity – and therefore casual clothes are the most appropriate (tracks suit, sweat shirt, jeans and sneakers, for example).

The sessions

Each session should contain:

Time	Item
10 mins	Exercise – warm ups – simple physical movement
15 mins	Movement – working together in twos/threes
20 mins	Script preparation – together, if many parts – in groups, if smaller sketches
10 mins	Break
30/40 mins	Script rehearsal
Variable	Prayers

The time can be scaled down if your drama activity is contained within the general evening. However, if it is, then you should not be preparing any lengthy presentation, like a three-act play. Only sketches and short plays should be within your material if you have less than two hours dedicated to drama rehearsal. Equally, if you are preparing with a major script, then at least two hours each meeting for preparation and rehearsal will be needed after the first read through and casting.

Do vary the movement/exercise routines and their length each week. You may like to introduce some mental or concentration exercises as an offset to the physical movement activities.

Remember that the most compelling and authentic presentations rely on immediately believable relationships between people enacting roles. The relationship comes first, and first, and first! All the movement and exercises are designed to train actors to relate naturally to each other – before assuming a character. More importantly, in a Christian group, is the development of fellowship and spiritual bonds (remember, we are all part of one body, the body of Christ).

Material

This will probably prove the most difficult exercise initially. But do not despair – help is at hand!

Firstly: at the end of this chapter you will find a Reading List of published books, most of which contain a selection of sketches, short plays, as well as more expansive instruction on Christian drama. The items are all based on providing a message – some direct, some indirect; and they do it in a variety of styles: serious, satirical, slapstick. Although these are identifiable as 'Christian' drama, they contain all the elements of secular drama, including all the challenges. If you begin with some of these sketches, and work carefully at them, following stage instructions, characterisation, etc. you will be building a solid experience and set of skills for your group to tackle wider texts. Bear in mind that some of the writers do make their living from drama performance and writing, and you must check the details for performing rights and licences. The fees are usually very modest.

Secondly: most libraries carry some drama works and compilations, and all libraries can get hold of particular volumes for you. If you are a new group, may I suggest that you limit your performance aims to sketches and short 'one acters' for the first two years? This will allow relationships to build, skills to emerge, talent to grow – and shake out those whose commitment was self-interest rather than service.

Thirdly: look local! You may find, on asking or putting a notice in the parish magazine, that some writers actually live in your area. They may have written in the past, and be prepared to have you perform their work (in some cases they may beat a path to your door, clutching fifty scripts).

A word of caution! You need to be very diplomatic in handling writers, would-be authors, and all who have the gleam of 'own performance' in their eye. If you receive very poor material, I suggest that you classify it to the author as 'unsuitable for your group at present'. This will save his or her feelings and your reputation.

Fourthly: why not write your own, as a group? You may find that one person has an idea for presentation, and that by kicking it around the basis of a script will emerge. It's a very enjoyable and constructive approach for small groups to create a sketch in this way. Often the process can be started by choosing a familiar story or theme, and illustrating it differently, by interpretation and visual presentation. Where do you find such familiar stories? Well, Christians have a ready made and almost inexhaustible source – the Bible. So . . .

Fifthly: use the Old and New Testament script! Our God is as much the God of drama as any other part of our lives and culture; therefore it should not be surprising to find the source of our belief to be also an endless source of expression. Whatever you choose – from Moses in the Bulrushes to Paul preaching to the Greeks in Athens – the range of events, and themes, and their messages, not to say the varied interpretations, is challenging enough for any drama group, new *or* existing. My own parish group in Surrey have been concentrating on Bible presentations for over two years – and we have not scratched the surface in what we could present, or would like to enact, in both church services and special drama evenings. Incidentally, many sketches are contained in the books referred to in the Reading List.

A last piece of advice on material – keep it simple. All your chosen works should be within reach of the talents of your group. It's risky thinking that you can present the Last Supper if you have, say, six girls and two men in the group. I say it's risky, because of course there are ways in which you could do this – but only using symbolic scenes and representative roles. That kind of drama needs long and careful preparation of skills within the actors.

Keep learning to a minimum, and concentrate on characterisation, on developing the people in the situation you are portraying. You may do well to enact narrated mime, at first. This allows the readers to have the words in front of them and the actors to concentrate on representing movement – emotions, reactions, atmosphere. Keep it simple.

An existing group?

You may already have a drama group. Great. Now that you have read this far (thank you), what do you do with the information you have? Can I suggest that you do a stocktake on your situation? What are your members like, your scripts, your performances, your fellowship? Is everything going the way you imagined? Well, the answer is usually: 'Yes, but . . .', or 'like the curate's egg – it's good in parts'. Let me say that much of what applies to a new group can be introduced to an existing team – with benefits all round. However, you may have grown and deepened the skills of the members to a point where you are ready for much more.

Taking further steps

I would suggest that, if this is the stage you feel you have brought your group to, one completely constructive action you should take is to pray. Asking God is always a faultless approach. There are also some pragmatic steps you can take.

1 Meet with the members for an informal evening – i.e. non-rehearsal. Start with prayer, then move into discussion of some of the directions you feel you'd like to take the group. Of course,

you should make this exacting and challenging, and not just change for change sake.

2 Note the views of the group. I mean, *write them down*, because you should rethink them after the meeting. Concentrate on those that are most commonly held – and which will cause the group to strengthen and grow.

3 Represent the results of the evening as a plan for, say, the next year: events, plays, sketches, groups within the group or whatever.

4 Lose no time in introducing the fresh ideas, through a detailed timetable of sessions. Remember, it's a lot like when you become a Christian. You should tell people – as many as you can, as soon as possible!

5 Monitor how things are going. How? By asking the actors of course.

YOUNG PEOPLE IN DRAMA

There are some special considerations for young people working in drama:

1 Some of the group may be short on patience and sustained interest. You will have to try and mature them gradually. You could do this by varying their involvement in each presentation. For example, in one they may have a leading part, in another they might help to write some of the script; yet another might call for the technical skills of sound or costume or props. By the way, redirecting an individual's involvement in production is one solution to the problem of someone who simply cannot act. If you have the embarrassment of telling someone that they will not be *in* the play, compromise by suggesting that their real contribution would be backstage.

2 At all levels, teenagers are acutely perceptive. All the scripts that you use, and all the work that you do, should be of as high a quality and as acceptable a performance as they would

expect from the professionals. Anyone who doesn't demand this standard of you, and give it back to the group, really needs to be helped to achieve those targets – or politely redirected to another interest.

3 Long term commitments are difficult to envisage when you are young, as are disciplines of rehearsal and work. You may have to confront their attitude on this very early on. I think you may find that the right time to do this is when you are casting. But be sure that you spell out absolutely clearly the time and effort you require from each person in preparing the play, or the sketches. Don't negotiate anything less than full acceptance of this, because those who are really interested will stick with you.

4 Many people tend at first to think of the situation serving their needs, their self-expression, their satisfactions, rather than the other way. In a Christian setting, you have the privilege of training young people early and turning their thinking round. Drama, really good drama, is a fusion of service and talent: service to the author and his script and to the audience, and hard won and worked at talent. The Christian should accept these principles 'in love'. And, of course, that love transforms – and it's a great joy to make that attitude grow in any youth group.

5 Finally, feedback. The older we are the more controlled we become in our emotions – sometimes to the point where it would be nice to be as natural as many people are. Especially in saying 'thanks'. Remember to go out of your way to give feedback to your group members – both thank you and well done (first please); and then help with areas that need improving. Of course, don't dissemble. Where someone is particularly weak in the team, seek to deal with this kindly, while building them up in other outlets where their talent will be a strength.

PERFORMANCES

Last, but not least, the performance. Like all the aspects I have touched on, there is too much to be said in one short section of one short chapter. However, I would like to give you some condensed advice.

Preparation

There can never be enough, but commonsense must prevail, or you will wear out both your actors and the freshness of any play.

As a rule of thumb, for short pieces (up to ten minutes), for each minute of performance you should be spending a total of from half to three-quarters of an hour in rehearsal of the piece – i.e. movement, words, stage business, final rehearsal. For longer plays, the preparation time is more like three-quarters of an hour for each minute on stage. So a one-hour drama will have 45 hours of rehearsal. Does that seem a lot? Well, just think! you have to allow for all the actors' rehearsals, plus costume, lighting, perhaps music, technical run-through and so on – and so on! Of course, as leader, producer, director, you will have to stand alongside your hard working team. In terms of your own commitment think of the number of rehearsal hours, and then add 50 per cent more for your own background preparation.

Casting

Don't overlook the age and condition of your actors and actresses. Make your casting decisions not just on ability to remember lines, or portray character, but also on relative age, looks, size; also the track record of the person for attendance and commitment. Be prepared to cast understudies at the start of rehearsal, and to use this as a means of motivating the lesser used members of the group.

Place and time

There are really no limits – rooms, church halls, churches, lawns, shopping centres, even garages. Drama is highly portable. And when? Well, it depends on your aims. If you are giving an evangelistic message, it may be within a service of worship, or as street theatre in a shopping centre. It may be complete entertainment you are providing, or it may be for children and families on someone's back lawn. Accept as many invitations as you feel you are able to do well. Youth evenings, clubs, speakers seeking illustrative drama, clergymen looking for 'live' sermons, church societies, Rotary Clubs, Christmas parties – the list is unlimited.

Costumes and props

Start simple. Many short pieces will require ordinary clothes (not distracting colours) and for this I suggest, dark trousers/skirt and light shirt/blouse, say white. This is especially effective doing mime with several people. If you need to attract visually (especially for children), use primary colours and larger-than-life styles of clothing. With props or stage furniture, it's surprising how imaginative your audience can be, so you can travel light for many presentations. Many lofts and spare bedroom wardrobes yield up a stock of good, multi-purpose items of clothing and hand props and stage furniture.

IN SUMMARY

A short recap of what you have read might best be achieved as Do's and Don'ts:

Do	– Pray	– always.
	Start simple	– with scripts and staging.
	Communicate well	– to would be members.
	Work consistently	– for high standards.
	Choose wisely	– in casting and performance.
	Show willing	– by listening and redirecting.
	Have patience	– with all actors/members of the group.
Don't	– Ask more	– than you would do yourself.
	Command	– so much as persuade and direct.
	Deceive	– about abilities.
	Ignore	– when suggestions and ideas come up.

If the above seems familiar as part of the Christian way of life, it is! Of course, it works well in every situation in your life, so why not in leading drama?

Lastly – enjoy it! Remember the many facets of God's personality that emerge in man, and mould those gifts together to make something worthy – for His glory.

All things come from you and of your own do we give you.

SUGGESTIONS FOR FURTHER READING AND DRAMA RESOURCES

P. Burbridge and M. Watts, *Lightning Sketches* (Hodder and Stoughton).
—, *Red Letter Days* (Hodder and Stoughton).
—, *Time to Act* (Hodder and Stoughton).
'Fisher-folk', *Building Worship Together* (Celebration).
Fraser Grace, *Little Black Paperback Book* (Kingsway Publications).
Peter Hamilton, *Amateur Stage Handbook* (Pitman and Sons).
Gordan and Ronni Lamont, *Move Yourselves* (Bible Society).
Martin Leach and Kevin Yell (compilers), *Act Justly* (Collins).
Geoffrey and Judith Stevenson, *Steps of Faith* – dance and movement (Kingsway Publications).
Steve and Janet Stickley, *Footnotes* (Hodder and Stoughton).
Watts, *Laughter in Heaven* (Marc Europe).
Using the Bible – in drama (Bible Society).

The list of drama books and sketches is considerable. Above are a number of books that have proved popular over many years. However, if you want any of the latest publications, visit your local Christian bookshop.

26
INSURANCE

Insurance is an area of youth work of which leaders need increasingly to be aware. Whether you are running a large open youth club from the church hall or a small group in someone's home, it is important that the group is adequately insured. Insurance may at times seem a very complex issue, but there are some simple precautions you can take so that you are covered in case of any accidents.

It is recommended that you talk to your church Treasurer or the person in your parish who deals with insurance. Find out exactly what cover the church has and how this relates to your group's membership and activities. It is important to outline the complete range of events that the club is involved with so that nothing is overlooked. For example, are you aware what the situation is if you take the group away for a weekend or simply on an outing?

Public Liability

Every club should be covered by Public Liability Insurance and the cover should extend to all leaders or those acting on behalf of the PCC or the legally constituted church body. Normally Public Liability is covered by the church's general policy so that your group should not need a separate policy. In case there is an accident and someone sues a youth leader rather than the church, the church's insurers will pay up on the basis of the Public Liability policy. The church should have this cover to protect all those who are involved in voluntary work of whatever kind.

But it is important to make sure that it *does* cover all the group leaders, for there may be restrictions on the age-limit and the total number of voluntary helpers on the policy. The policy should also include member-to-member liability, so as to cover accidents between individual members of the group. If changes need to be made to the policy, then the appropriate action should be taken.

You should also be aware of what activities are covered, since some hazardous games or ventures may not be included. So, if you are going rock-climbing, playing football or organising an event on the public highway, additional cover will probably be needed.

Group Personal Accident

There is no legal requirement for such cover to be provided, although it is a very good idea. This cover provides for compensation if leaders or group members are killed or injured while taking part in group activities. Such a policy will cover someone who loses money because they are unable to work due to injury. Remember that breaking a bone can be very easy, and it can happen during the most routine activities. The result may be a number of months off work if the break is a complex fracture. This type of policy varies in its cost and is dependent on the type of activities your group carries out.

Fire, Theft and All-Risks

Check the cover held by the owners of the property that you use. The policy cover may just be for Fire and Theft, or it may be a separate All-Risks policy. If you meet on church premises, the situation should be straightforward. However, if the property is owned by another body, check to what extent you are liable for damage. It may be necessary to send details of the property, and the extent of your liability for damage, to the insurance company responsible for cover. The policy should cover equipment and furnishings; but if you have a particularly expensive item, make sure it is named and insured for the necessary amount. It may also be necessary for the policy to be extended if any of the equipment is to be used away from the main premises. Also, check if the insurance company imposes any maximum financial limits to its cover.

If you borrow or hire something – a video camera, for instance – you may need to arrange for temporary insurance cover.

Personal Effects and Monies

Cover of this type indemnifies voluntary helpers for loss or damage of personal effects only. It is probably better, though, that such matters are covered through the individual's personal insurance policy.

Money that is stolen or misappropriated on the premises should be covered through the policy of the property owners.

Cover for Weekends and Holidays

If you are taking your group away, you will probably need to extend your insurance cover, particularly if you are borrowing or hiring equipment and renting premises. Your insurance company will usually want to see a copy of any hiring agreement. Special insurance cover will obviously be required if you are going abroad, and also if you are involved in any particular events or sports.

As the leader you will be responsible for the group, so check your legal liability cover. If you are also responsible for group finances, you may want cover for loss of money.

Employer's Liability

This form of insurance will apply only in the case of those employed by the club or church. But since an increasing number of churches are employing full-time youth workers, they must have an Employer's Liability policy. This is a statutory requirement. If someone is employed by the local authority, then that body is responsible. A certificate verifying the current validity of the policy should be displayed in a prominent place on the premises used. The policy covers persons employed by the club who have an accident while carrying out their duties.If an accident is the result of the employer's negligence, the

employer can be sued. Claims can be made for as much as
£500,000.

Vehicle insurance

See chapter 29, on Transport, below.

Additional cover

If additional cover is necessary for your youth group beyond
that provided by the policy held by your church authorities,
then it is worth approaching one of the following:
- The Ecclesiastical Insurance Office Ltd, Beaufort House,
  Brunswick Road, Gloucester GL1 1JZ.
- Youth Clubs U.K., 11 St Bride's Street, London EC4A 4AS.
  Tel. 071 353 2366
- A local insurance broker who will give you free advice on
  the range of policies available, and obtain for you
  competitive quotations.

Many Diocesan Youth Officers operate a Diocesan Insurance
Scheme for Youth Groups, so do contact your Officer.

The information given in this chapter is correct to the best
of the knowledge of the author. No liability can be accepted
for any errors of detail.

27
GOING PLACES

Having just returned from running a week-long houseparty, I thought I should sit down and write the chapter on 'Going Places'. Those of you who have taken a group away for a weekend or a whole week will need no convincing of how important such an undertaking is. Those of you who have not done so, well, I'm afraid you have missed out on a great deal. But fear not: now is the time to get your act together and start thinking about taking your youth group off somewhere.

For years I have been involved in taking groups of young people away. The groups have varied in size from 16 to 450. They have varied in their nature – from youth groups to confirmation classes, to groups of individuals from different churches. The styles of the occasions have also varied – from camps to a weekend on a theme at a small retreat centre, to taking over a boarding school with an activity based houseparty. The more I am involved in taking groups away, the more convinced I am of the value of the idea.

VALUE OF CAMPS AND HOUSEPARTIES

Fellowship

This can start the moment everyone arrives at the church hall and piles into the minibus to go off, or the moment you arrive at your destination. Everyone will be naturally in high spirits and looking forward to the weekend. Hopefully that will include yourself. A weekend or week away gives the opportunity for a good dose of fellowship. The teenagers will get to know each other at a far deeper level. As the weekend develops, they will become more relaxed and open with each other. Some of the barriers which were never lowered at a youth group meeting disappear. They relate to each other as real friends. In fact, sitting in front of me is a letter which arrived in today's post from a thirteen-year-old who was on last week's houseparty. He says that he's never been away with a more friendly group of people. That's encouraging, because the majority did not know each other before the week began.

In fact, I'm often amazed and pleasantly encouraged when I look back on a week and realise that I had never heard a word said in anger or an argument take place. Maybe a camp or houseparty also teaches tolerance, which is an important aspect of fellowship. Honesty also usually comes from the experience. Because people are relaxed and open they become honest about what they think and feel. They will more readily talk about their doubts and concerns. This will then give the youth leader the opportunity to minister in a more meaningful way to the young person. Fellowship becomes a real experience and avoids the superficiality that can often hamper effective work with teenagers.

Leader–teenager relations

The youth leader is provided with a wonderful opportunity really to get to know the teenagers in the group. Through whatever activity you are doing the young people will have the chance to relate to you in a more meaningful way. Seeing you first thing in the morning may not be a pretty experience, but it is a very different context from an evening at the church hall or parish room. They will get to know more of you, and you of them. If you think about a weekend away, there are a lot of occasions where the young will see you in different circumstances. Some weeks ago I was helping to lead a week with a group from a particular parish. It just so happened that one of the young girls in the group used to attend a school where I regularly took morning assembly. She was used to seeing me in jacket and dog-collar, in a formal setting with the headmaster and school staff. At the end of the week's camp she wrote to me and said that she now saw me in a completely different light. Usually the contrast for a youth leader will not be as striking as this particular occasion, but the way you appear to the group will be different and more varied. If you take your family with you, the young people will see how you treat and relate to your wife, or husband and children. This can be an even greater witness than all the words spoken about relationships and respect.

It is to be hoped, also, that the event will also encourage a sense of respect for you as the teenagers see you at a deeper level. There should be a Christian integrity about the kind of person you are, your convictions and values, as they see you handle people in circumstances that demand teamwork. Mind you, respect is a two-way thing and it also involves your respecting them as individuals. I find the best way to relate to teenagers is to treat them and respect them as adults. If you treat them as adults they will usually behave in a mature and adult manner.

Atmosphere

You can create a very powerful and positive atmosphere over a weekend. It is fostered by some of the things that we have already mentioned. But atmosphere and feeling are in themselves very important statements about who we are, what we believe and what we feel about God and each other. The atmosphere may be a little 'starchy' at first. Folk are possibly feeling a little tense before they become immersed in the experience. If you are able to contrast the first hour of your camp and the last hour, the atmosphere of each is usually quite different. This sense of atmosphere and 'feel' was particularly brought home to me when I had to leave a camp for a couple of days. I left late after the talk on a Tuesday night and returned early on the Friday morning. The development of the atmosphere in the intervening period was quite noticeable. People were more relaxed, relating to each other more meaningfully, spiritually more aware. I was able to see the contrast more clearly because I had stepped out of the situation and then returned at another point.

The value of a good atmosphere and its development are noticed and registered either consciously or unconsciously. One clergyman, arriving to pick up his son from a houseparty remarked after the final group photograph session, 'What a lovely atmosphere.' Such things are important!

Teaching

Because of the obviously greater length of time that is spent together over a weekend than is possible in ordinary club meetings, the opportunity for teaching is unique. You may be able to achieve up to five or six sessions without running the risk of making the weekend too 'heavy'. In addition, activities such as discussion groups or workshops and seminars may follow on. A weekend away provides an opportunity to get really stuck into a particular theme or to understand an aspect of Christian discipleship. Such a teaching opportunity can be more effective than many months of group meetings and talks.

Worship

Given the dynamics of all that we have mentioned, there is clearly an opportunity for a very rich sense and experience of worship. The rather pathetic singing of a Sunday night meeting can develop into something that is more expressive and meaningful. Taking Communion as an informal sharing of the bread and wine in a spiritual climax to the weekend can gain greater power than is normally experienced in the rather formal service in church. In fact, your experience of the Eucharist as part of your worship during the weekend may resemble more the Last Supper than any Sunday morning Communion service held in church. Worship is fundamental and it needs to be high in the priority of any residential experience. We do not worship God because of what we can get out of it: we worship Him because of who He is. The opportunities for worship will encourage the young person to see God and feel the presence of His love.

Group momentum

What does a weekend away do for any group? It creates a sense of belonging and identity. It also gives the group a momentum which is crucial to its common activity. Any group needs such an occasion to breathe life back into itself, so that the energy and emotional power of the group are rekindled. Where this is created the group will have the momentum to keep going week by week until the next significant event. The momentum of the group will affect a whole range of things – the numbers that attend it, its sense of enjoyment, its desire to do new things, and its concern to invite outsiders to share in the experience.

Overall, more can be achieved in a weekend – or better still, a week away – than many, many months of regular meetings. So get to it!

PRELIMINARY DECISIONS

First of all, decide as a group what type of weekend you want and what kind of 'accommodational environment would suit your needs'. You should also, at a very early stage, decide how much is considered a reasonable amount to pay, and what is the best time of year for your members to join this kind of activity.

The type of weekend could be that provided by:

- Christian residential centre;
- a youth hostel;
- a County Council residential centre;
- a church hall;
- a camp site;
- a school.

A *residential centre*

There are Christian residential centres all over the country, varying enormously in shape and size and amenities. The surprising thing is how many there are. You could almost write a book on the centres that are available.

207

Some dioceses have their own residential centres for youth groups. These again vary in their amenities. Some have a full-time warden who does all the cooking; bedrooms are individual and the ambience is akin to that of a cheap hotel. Other diocesan centres are in converted churches, sleeping is in dormitories and cooking is done by the group itself. Of course, costs vary.

Youth hostel

There are some 250 excellent youth hostels around the country. If you are a member of the Youth Hostels Association (YHA, Trevelyan House, St Stephen's Hill, St Albans, Herts AL1 2OY), it is worth contacting them and discussing the possibility of taking a group to a particular centre. If you take a group out of season, you may find you have the hostel to yourselves. Because the hostels are usually situated in good geographical locations, it can be easy to organise walks and outings for the weekend.

A County Council residential centre

It is worth contacting the Youth Section of your County Council. Some county organisations have residential centres specifically for young people. They are usually well-equipped and cheap to hire.

A church hall

Some churches are very happy to have their premises used by groups. The advantage is that they are very cheap to hire, and the clergy and churchfolk may prove very helpful and co-operative in a variety of ways. There may, however, be dis-advantages in regard to sleeping arrangements and cooking facilities, and these aspects require careful consideration at the outset.

How do you find out about such things? Well, speak to your denominational youth officer or your local clergy. Your priest or pastor may be able to recommend a previous parish or church community they have served in, or know of suitable premises in the charge of one of their colleagues elsewhere.

You could use the occasion to visit and develop links with the young people in that Christian community. They, in turn, could come and visit you for a weekend. Could be great!

A *camp*

In the summertime camping is an easy possibility. Easy, that is, if you have got the equipment and are prepared to put up with the British weather. Some centres already have the sites and tents in place, and you simply arrive with your group and the leadership-cum-cooking team. Another possibility is to use a farmer's field. That, of course, would require previous negotiation.

If you are intending a camping weekend, it is important to organise the logistics carefully. For example, you will need to check the following aspects:

- toilet facilities;
- acquiring tents;
- adequate cover in case of bad weather;
- a mess tent for cooking and eating;
- cooking equipment and storage of perishables;
- lighting;
- chairs and tables;
- electricity supply, power or fuel for cooking and heating.

If you need to borrow tents or a marquee, contact the local Scouts or Guides – they are usually very happy to help and give advice.

A *school*

If you are a large youth group, or indeed if you have strong contacts with groups in your area, you may want to consider hiring a school with all its facilities for a week. Why not be ambitious? With a school you can take as many teenagers as you want and most of your activity-needs will be on site. Some schools which are church foundations look favourably on Christian youth groups and are happy for the income. However, for every twenty letters you may write to a headmaster or headmistress, you may get only one or two positive replies. Even so, the idea is well worth exploring.

Cost

Working out the actual cost of your weekend away is crucial. If you are attempting such a venture for the first time, it may be worth discussing with your vicar or church leader whether any loss can be underwritten by the church. The reason for this is that any camp or houseparty that is attempted for the first time is likely to produce costs which may not have been allowed for. Also you may have problems with the numbers who participate, which will affect the finance. Calculating how many teenagers may attend a weekend can be a nightmare, particularly if there is no tradition of going away in the church's youth work. If some key members of your group decided to attend, most of the rest will come. If they don't – well, your group will be smaller. But don't be despondent if you get a small turn-out. Those who do attend will go back and tell everybody what a great time they had, and next year you will find you have little trouble in persuading people to come.

If you are going to a residential centre, you need to be very clear as to what financial penalties are involved if numbers fall below your expectation, or indeed if you have to cancel.

What do you have to budget for with a weekend? The following should certainly figure in your reckoning:

- Cost of the centre;
- Catering;
- Transportation;
- Outings;
- Speaker's expenses, if you are inviting an outside speaker;
- Administrative expense, relating to postage and publicity material.

Time of year

Traditionally a lot of groups go away during the summer, but there are advantages in holding weekends at other times of the year. An obvious one is avoidance of a clash with family holidays. But if you do decide on an autumn or spring houseparty, take care to check with the various headteachers of your teenagers that the date does not conflict with such school events as examinations, field-trips, sports days, plays and concerts, etc. Also check that it does not conflict with an important church event.

ORGANISING THE WEEKEND'S PATTERN

The spiritual theme

You may wish to choose a theme for the weekend which relates to how you develop the spiritual programme and its content. You could choose any theme you want, but the following offer appropriate possibilities:

- an Old Testament or New Testament book;
- a particular aspects of Jesus' teaching;
- a character or series of characters from the Bible;
- a theological issue such as Salvation, Grace, Divine Love or Realised Eschatology (well, that's probably a bit too heavy for teenagers!);
- issues of social concern, and how a Christian should respond to them.

You may wish to invite a speaker to come with his or her own spiritual programme, although most speakers usually like to be given a subject, since the choice of what you give them will tell them something about the group. The advantage of a speaker is that the young people will tend to listen more readily to someone different. The face, the voice, the person is unfamiliar so they will be interested in what the speaker has to say. If briefed well by you, the speaker should be aware of the things that have concerned and affected the group over the recent months.

Programme of events

There is a wide variety of ways you can put together a programme for a weekend. Virtually each group will have its own ideas. But here is an outline of a fairly typical weekend away. Incidentally, you may wish to put together an attractive programme to give each person on arrival which shows what is happening and when.

Friday night

7.30 Arrival
8.00 Dinner
9.00 Introduction and ice-breaker games
9.30 Worship and Session I
10.30 Evening Drink (hot chocolate, etc.)
11.00 Bed or late-night video (depending on how strict you are and on the age of your group)

Saturday

8.00 Wakey Wakey (i.e. Get Up)
8.30 Breakfast
9.30 Session II
11.00 Coffee
11.30 Session III
1.00 Lunch
2.30 Outside activity – swimming, ice-skating, ramble, ten-pin bowling, etc.
5.00 Tea
5.30 Indoor games – table-tennis, snooker or what you have organised
7.00 Dinner
8.00 Session IV
9.00 Disco, Concern or Barbecue
11.00 Bed or Video

Sunday

8.00 Arise and Shine
8.30 Breakfast
10.00 Planning the Morning Worship (involving everyone in drama, dance, prayers, reading, music, communion, etc.)

11.00 Coffee
11.30 Morning Worship (Session V)
 1.00 Lunch
 2.00 Closing Session VI
 3.30 Clear up
 4.00 Tea
 4.30 Depart
 6.30 Evensong service in home church. (This can help
        the process of integration with the church and also
        have the effect of informing the congregation of
        what the young people have been doing.)

ADMINISTRATION

A popular residential centre will need to be booked at least a year in advance. Other administrative issues to be handled are:

- Letters to parents;
- Parental consent forms (if the young people are below the age of eighteen);
- Booking forms;
- Insurance for the weekend;
- List of items for the young people to bring;
- Publicity (parish magazine, posters – perhaps local press);
- Deposits;
- Organising the leaders and cooks!

Where to go

If you are used to taking a group away, you probably have a favourite location; but it is still worth keeping an eye open to other possibilities, because other centres may have better facilities.

Helpful contacts

The following individuals and organisations can offer invaluable advice:

- Your denominational Youth Officer.
- County Council Youth Office in your area.
- Chairman, Residential Training Centre Wardens' Conference, c/o The General Synod Board of Education, Church House, Dean's Yard, London SW1P 3NZ.

(This organisation will supply you with a brochure of about 28 centres for young people throughout the country.)

- Christian Camping International (UK) Ltd, PO Box 169, Coventry CV5 9QR.

(They publish a comprehensive brochure on accommodation in Britain.)

- UK Christian Handbook: available from The Bible Society, Stonehill Green, Westlea, Swindon, Wilts SN5 7PG.

Also check organisations listed in the Appendix of National Addresses, below.

SUGGESTIONS FOR FURTHER READING

Janet Lumb, *Know How to Run Young People's Groups and Houseparties* (Scripture Union).
Arlo Reichter, *Get Away* (Bible Society).

28
YOUNG PEOPLE AND THE LAW

It is possible that, as a youth leader, you may occasionally be involved in a situation that requires a certain amount of legal knowledge. Here it is wise to operate with extreme care. The whole area of law is a very complex one, and aspects of it can change over the course of time. Below are some guidelines for the present situation as regards teenagers and the law.

A Teenager aged 13:

- Is able to be employed on a part-time basis. There are very severe restrictions on the nature of the employment, particularly in relation to the number of hours that may be worked. A teenager over 13 who is charged with an offence can have his/her fingerprints taken either by consent or after a magistrate's order.

Aged 14:

- May enter licensed premises provided he/she is accompanied by someone who is 18 or older. However, they are not allowed to buy or consume alcohol.
- Can be sent to a Detention Centre.
- May apply for a firearms certificate.

Aged 15:

- May watch a '15' rated movie.
- Can be sent to a Youth Custody Centre.

Aged 16:

- May enter licensed premises on his/her own, but is not allowed to consume alcohol.

- May ride a motorcycle or moped which is not greater than 50 cc.
- May open a current account at a bank.
- May leave school and work up to 48 hours per week, but not at night. Earnings belong to the teenager, not to the parents.
- May marry with parental consent.
- May engage in sexual intercourse, but not homosexual.
- Is able to enter a mental hospital as a voluntary patient.
- Is able to consent to medical, surgical and dental treatment.
- May buy fireworks.
- May, if male, apply to join the armed services with parental consent.
- Can be given a Community Service Order.
- May be admitted to the electoral roll of a church.

Aged 17:

- May, on passing required test, hold a licence to drive an automobile or certain categories of commercial vehicle, as well as an agricultural tractor.
- Is able to buy firearms.
- May hold a private pilot's licence.
- May, if female, apply to join the armed services, but only with parental consent.
- Can have his/her name published in reports of court proceedings, which will now be in the magistrates' rather than the juvenile courts. Liable to be sent to prison.

Aged 18 (legally an adult):

- May buy and consume alcohol on licensed premises.
- May marry without parental consent.
- May buy and sell property.
- May apply for a passport without parental consent.
- Is eligible for entry in the electoral register and for voting in local, parliamentary and European elections.
- May enter a gambling establishment.
- May be admitted to watch an '18' rated movie.
- May enter into a consumer credit agreement.

- May make a valid will.
- Is liable to pay full National Insurance contributions.
- Is entitled to bring and defend a legal action in court under his/her own name.
- Is eligible to sit on a Parochial Church Council.

For further details consult *Enfranchisement: Young People and the Law* – a guide to the law as it affects young people, which is available from the National Youth Agency. (See the Appendix of National Addresses below.)

If in doubt, the advice of a friendly solicitor can be very valuable. Also check with the Police or the Citizens Advice Bureau or a Legal Advice Centre.

YOUTH GROUPS AND THE LAW

As the youth leader you have a responsibility not only to the young people, but also to the parents. The parents have an expectation that you will exercise care over their children. This obviously involves their safety and personal well-being. If an accident happens either inside or outside the club, are you covered by insurance if you are held responsible for the group? Read the chapter 26, above, on Insurance.

It is also worth remembering that the group, and by implication the leader, will be held responsible for members' behaviour before and after the club meeting and for any trouble in bus shelters, telephone kiosks or lounging around on walls. This may not be strictly illegal behaviour, but could be deemed to be causing a nuisance, and it will certainly affect relationships between the group and outside agencies such as the police, local residents and individuals.

Most youth groups meet on church property so any limitations from a legal point of view are not a problem, but . . .

A Music, Singing and Dancing licence

The church hall that you use should already have a licence of this kind. But if you plan to hold a concert or a club disco, do check the hall's licence because it will tell you how many people may be admitted and the various fire precautions that are necessary. If a licence is required for an event you are staging, it is issued by the local authority.

Films

A licence is not needed if a film is to be shown to club members. However, if non-members are present a licence is needed.

Street procession, march of witness

If you are planning a march of witness at Easter, or some special occasion that involves public roads, etc., you must inform the police. You will generally find they are co-operative, and because of their experience in these matters will give you some helpful advice.

Posters

Putting up posters in a public place is called fly-posting and, as you are probably aware, is illegal. However, if the youth activity that you are organising is a non-commercial event, then you may be able to display posters under certain circumstances – for example, *if:*

- You have the owner's consent to use his house or fence.
- Your poster is not larger than 6 square feet.
- No view of the road is obscured.
- You comply with the local bye-laws.

Money collections

House-to-house collections, or indeed street collections involving money, need a police permit. The details for this can be obtained from the local authority.

Performing Rights

Any youth group which allows recorded or live music to be played at its meetings and events should have a licence from the Performing Rights Society. Enquiries in connection with this should be made to: The Performing Rights Society, Copyright House, 29–33 Berners Street, London W1P 4AA.

Raffles

These are usually permissible if tickets are sold at a single event and the prizes are not cash or alcohol. Other requirements are that the raffle should not be the main attraction of the event and that the tickets be sold only on the premises. If in doubt, check with the local police. The regulations governing Lotteries, with sale of tickets to the general public outside the individual event, are much stricter.

Working with the local police

It is very important in running a club or group to make contact with the local police. They are often keen to know about community groups for young people and will generally be interested and supportive of what is happening. In the majority of church groups the teenagers probably will feel no antagonism towards the police, so a mutually beneficial relationship can grow. You may want to invite someone from the local station either to come and speak to the group or just make a casual visit. Alternatively, the group could make a visit to the station. The police often have specialist skills, so a policewoman dealing with self-defence may be a useful evening's programme. Or you might get someone to speak about drugs.

In some areas of the country, however, and in particular in the cities, the relationship between the police and the young people is very often one of suspicion. A youth leader may have the opportunity to help in the healing process and bring together in greater understanding and trust the young and the police. This can be an uphill struggle, but it is one of the priorities a leader should have in mind.

Police powers

The police have the power to stop and search if they have grounds for suspicion that the individual or group

- is in possession of drugs;
- is carrying firearms;
- has on the person goods that have been stolen.

The police can be asked about the reason for their search, but it is unwise to resist being searched as this could lead to a charge of 'obstructing a policeman in the execution of his duty'.

The police, of course, also have the power to arrest and take someone in for questioning. A young person is best advised never to resist arrest as any physical conflict can only make the matter worse. Whatever the situation, it is best that the teenager should co-operate. Young people may be asked to go to the police station without actually being arrested. However, they can ask whether or not they are being placed under arrest and if so, for what reason. If young persons are in serious trouble, it may be in their interests not to answer any questions or sign any statements until they have seen a lawyer. Teenagers under the age of seventeen should be questioned in the presence of a parent or guardian.

A person being arrested has the right to have one person informed of this and the place of his or her detention.

If arrested, the police may release them on bail until their case is heard by the magistrates. Unless the offence is serious, the police must release them if they cannot be brought before the magistrate within 24 hours (48 hours at weekends). Prisoners under seventeen must be given bail unless there is a strong reason for not doing so. If the police are prepared to release them, they will be asked to agree in writing to appear at court on a certain day and to pay a specified sum if they fail to do so. The police may also ask for a guarantee from other people that they will pay a specified amount of money if the young person does not turn up in court.

SUGGESTED READING

Enfranchisement: Young People and the Law, produced by the National Youth Agency (see list of addresses).

29
TRANSPORT

If you are organising a trip out, avoid just using cars! Why?
Because it detracts from the fun and fellowship of the occasion.
If you are going out either on some activity or to an event,
the experience starts the moment everyone gathers in the car-
park. But if you put everyone into cars, the atmosphere usually
is broken up because the group is split up!

This was well illustrated to me when one year we were having
a 'beach bar-b-que'. The idea was pretty stupid because the
beach was sixty odd miles away! But we hired a double-decker
bus; with a driver, of course, and made for the coast. We left
around 6.00 p.m., arrived on the beach at 7.30, went
swimming, played football and rounders. We then had our
barbecue followed by singing. The singing continued all the
way home and we arrived back around 11 o'clock. It was a
great occasion. The weather was typically British but no one
seemed to care. However, I failed to understand the lessons
involved in the activity. When we decided to do it again I could
not get the transport because I had left it too late to book. So
I decided a fleet of cars would be just as good. It wasn't. The
evening was not a failure – it's just that it did not have the
atmosphere and sense of fun and occasion. But I had learnt
my lesson. If you take a group somewhere, try if humanly
possible to keep them together. You don't have to hire a double-
decker bus or a coach – a minibus is just as good, but certain
legal requirements do need consideration.

If you have trouble getting hold of a minibus, have you tried
all the possibilities? For example:

- The local Youth Service Office;
- The Lions Club;
- Rotary;
- The local school, particularly if it is a church school;
- Any of the local churches;
- Scouts or Guides;
- Hiring one.

If you do have problems in getting a minibus, you will probably be surprised to find, if you ring around or simply ask, that there are usually quite a lot available for use. I frequently come across 'yet another' organisation which has a minibus, and usually they are happy to lend it out.

However, using a minibus means complying with certain legal requirements.

MINIBUS AND LEGAL REGULATIONS

Under the Road Traffic Act, a minibus may not be used for 'hire or reward' unless:

(i) it is licensed as a 'Public Service Vehicle';
(ii) the vehicle has a permit issued under the Minibus Act;
(iii) the vehicle is licensed as a 'Community Bus'.

'Hire or reward'

The law makes a distinction between carrying passengers free and for 'hire or reward'. However, the legal definition of 'hire or reward' is very strict. If your passengers — in other words, members of the youth group — pay directly or indirectly, then this is considered to be for 'hire or reward'. Also the definition regards 'hire or reward' as embracing payment for petrol, payment for the entrance to an event with travel included in the price, and subscription to a club which provides transport directly related to specific trips.

Minibus as a Public Service Vehicle

A PSV is a vehicle adapted to carry eight or more people and operating under the 'hire or reward' definitions. The requirements for a PSV are very strict on the fitness of vehicle holding a licence. The drivers will each need a PSV licence as well as the operating body.

Minibus as a community bus

A community bus is one which operates as a local bus service for the welfare needs of the community without making a profit.

Minibus permits

Permits are issued:

a) for vehicles carrying more than 7 but not more than 16 places for passengers;

b) for non-profit-making activities concerned with education, religion, social welfare, etc.;

c) for vehicles which comply with the Minibus (Conditions of Fitness, Equipment and Use) Regulations. These specify that the vehicle must be both equipped *and constructed* in certain distinct ways (e.g., Ford minibus require an extra pack to be fitted, available from the manufacturers);

d) for a specified vehicle. *Note:* one permit is required for each vehicle and for each organisation using it;

e) by designated organisations or by the Traffic Office.

A free guide for voluntary groups about the use of minibuses is available from the Traffic Commissioners at your local County Hall. The guide is entitled *Passenger Transport Provided by Voluntary Groups* (PSV 385).

POINTS TO CONSIDER

You may own or hire a minibus and use it for 'hire or reward' or for 'free'; but it is important to be fully aware of the following points:

1 Make sure your vehicle complies with the Road Safety and recent Minibus Acts. The vehicle must be properly insured.

Check all the details that relate to the insurance situation with your use of the vehicle.

2 Make sure your insurance company is aware of all the facts.

3 The vehicle must have a current MOT, be taxed and also be roadworthy.

4 You must comply with United Kingdom driving regulations which relate to driving hours and daily rest periods. Failure to comply can result in a heavy fine.

5 If you intend to drive on the Continent, there are considerable added complications. For information, contact:

The Bus and Coach Council (tel. 071 831 7546);
Regional office of the Automobile Association (AA);
Embassy or Tourist Office of the country concerned.

6 If you need to apply for a licence in connection with using a minibus, you should contact the Clerk to the Licensing Authority.

Legal responsibility

It is extremely important to be aware that responsibility for ensuring that all the legal requirements have been met rests with the hirer, not the hire company. So the onus is on you. If you use a minibus without complying with all the legal requirements, you could be prosecuted, fined, lose your licence, or even be imprisoned. Also, your insurance company may not pay compensation.

Driving hours in Britain

For the current legal regulations contact the Traffic Commissioners for your area.

USING YOUR CAR

If you use your car for transporting teenagers to an event, check with your insurance company that you do have adequate insurance cover. Because of the nature of the use, you may find you have to extend your cover.

TRAFFIC AREAS AND TRAFFIC AREA ADDRESSES

All correspondence should be addressed to the Clerk to the Licensing Authority, Traffic Commissioners.

Traffic Area	*Areas covered*	*Office address*
Scottish	Scotland	83 Princes Street Edinburgh EH2 2ER Tel: 031 225 5494 Fax: 031 225 5494 ext 312
North Eastern	Cleveland Durham Humberside North Yorkshire Northumberland Nottinghamshire South Yorkshire Tyne and Wear West Yorkshire	Hillcrest House 386 Harehills Lane Leeds LS9 6NF Tel: 0532 833533 Fax: 0532 489607
Eastern	Bedfordshire Buckinghamshire Cambridgeshire Essex Hertfordshire Leicestershire Lincolnshire Norfolk Northamptonshire Suffolk	Terrington House 13–15 Hills Road Cambridge CB2 1NP Tel: 0223 358922 Fax: 0223 358922 ext 2110
North Western	Cheshire Clwyd Cumbria Derbyshire Greater Manchester Gwynedd Lancashire Merseyside	Portcullis House Seymour Grove Stretford Manchester M16 0NE Tel: 061 872 5077 Fax: 061 848 7322

West Midland	Hereford and Worcester Shropshire Staffordshire Warwickshire West Midlands	Cumberland House 200 Broad Street Birmingham B15 1TD Tel: 021 631 3300 Fax: 021 631 3300 ext 415
South Wales	Dyfed Gwent Powys Mid Glamorgan South Glamorgan West Glamorgan	Caradog House 1–6 St Andrews Place Cardiff C1 3PW Tel: 0222 394027 Fax: 0222 371675
Western	Avon Berkshire Cornwall Devon Dorset Gloucestershire Hampshire Isle of Wight Oxfordshire Somerset Wiltshire	The Gaunts' House Denmark Street Bristol BS1 5DR Tel: 0272 755000 Fax: 0272 755055
South Eastern and Metropolitan	Kent Surrey East Sussex West Sussex Administrative area of Greater London	Ivy House 3 Ivy Terrace Eastbourne BN21 4QT Tel: 0323 21471 Fax: 0323 21057

When you contact your Traffic Commissioners' office you will be sent booklet PSV 385, *Passenger Transport Provided by Voluntary Groups*, which is very useful.

If you own your own minibus you should have a copy of *Your Minibus – is it legal?*, available from the Community Transport Association, 1A Old Street, Hyde, Cheshire, SK14 1LJ (Tel. 061 351 1475).

APPENDIX
NATIONAL ADDRESSES

CHRISTIAN YOUTH ORGANISATIONS AND AGENCIES

Baptist Union of Great Britain
Baptist House, PO Box 44, 129 Broadway, Didcot, Oxon
OX11 8RT
Tel. 0235 512077.

Catholic Youth Services
Southwell House, 39 Fitzjohn's Avenue, London NW3 5UT
Tel. 071 435 3596

Church of England Youth Services
National Youth Office, Church House, Westminster, London
SW1P 3NZ
Tel. 071 222 9011.

Church Youth Fellowship Association & Pathfinders
Athena Drive, Tachbrook Park, Warwick CV34 6NG
Tel. 0926 334242

The Council of Churches for Britain and Ireland
Youth Office, Inter-Church House, 35–41 Lower Marsh,
London SE1 7RL
Tel. 071 620 4444

Crusaders
2 Romeland Hill, St Albans, Hertfordshire AL3 4ET
Tel. 0727 55422

Frontier Youth Trust
130 City Road, London EC1V 2NJ
Tel. 071 250 1966

Methodist Association of Youth Clubs
2 Chester House, Pages Lane, Muswell Hill, London N10 1PR
Tel. 081 444 9845

Oasis Trust
Haddon Hall, 22 Tower Bridge Road, London SE1 4TR
Tel. 071 231 4583

Operation Mobilisation
The Quinta, Weston Rhym, Oswestry, Shropshire SY10 7LR
Tel. 0691 773388

Scripture Union
130 City Road, London EC1V 2NJ
Tel. 071 250 1966

United Reformed Church Youth Office
86 Tavistock Place, London WC1H 9RT
Tel. 071 837 7661

Youth For Christ
Cleobury Place, Cleobury Mortimer, Kidderminster, Worcestershire DY14 8JG
Tel. 0299 271158

Youth With A Mission
13 Highfield Oval, Ambrose Lane, Harpenden, Herts AL5 4BX
Tel. 0582 765481

VOLUNTARY CHRISTIAN WORK

There are a number of organisations which use volunteers for periods of service. If some of your young people are considering taking time off and want to be involved in Christian work, you may wish to contact the organisations listed below.

Ashburnham Christian Trust
Resident Director, Ashburnham Place, Battle, E. Sussex TN33 9NF

Birmingham City Mission
126 Arden Road, Acocks Green, Birmingham B27 6AG

Careforce
130 City Road, London EC1V 2NJ

Church Missionary Society
Partnership House, 157 Waterloo Road, London SE1 8UU

Crusaders
2 Romeland Hill, St Albans, Herts AL2 4ET

Latin Link
Whitefield House, 186 Kennington Park Road, London SE11 4BT

Oasis Trust
Haddon Hall, 22 Tower Bridge Road, London SE1 4TR

Operation Mobilisation
The Quinta, Weston Rhym, Oswestry, Shropshire SY10 7LT

Overseas Missionary Fellowship
Belmont, The Vine, Sevenoaks, Kent TN13 3TZ

Pioneer T.I.E. Teams
PO Box 79c, Esher, Surrey KT10 9LP

Soap Box Expeditions
14–15 Queens Road, Guildford, Surrey GU1 4JJ

South American Missionary Society
Allen Gardiner House, Pembury Road, Tunbridge Wells, Kent TN2 3QU

Task Force
Baptist Union, Baptist House, PO Box 44, 129 Broadway, Didcot, Oxon OX11 8RT

TEAR Fund
100 Church Road, Teddington, Middlesex TW11 8SY

Time for God
2 Chester House, Pages Lane, Muswell Hill, London N10 1PR

United Society for the Propagation of the Gospel (USPG)
Partnership House, 157 Waterloo Road, London SE1 8XA

World Vision
8 Abington Street, Northampton NN1 2AJ

Youth For Christ
Cleobury Place, Cleobury Mortimer, Worcestershire DY14 8JG

Youth With A Mission (YWAM)
13 Highfield Oval, Ambrose Lane, Harpenden, Herts AL5 4BX

OTHER YOUTH ORGANISATIONS

British Youth Council
57 Charlton Street, London NW1 1HU
Tel. 071 387 7559

Guide Association
17 Buckingham Palace Road, London SW1W 0PT
Tel. 071 834 6242

National Council for Voluntary Youth Services
3 Coborn Road, Bow, London E3 2DA

National Youth Agency
17–23 Albion Street, Leicester LE1 6GD
Tel. 0533 471200

The Prince's Trust
8 Bedford Row, London WC1R 4BU
Tel. 071 430 0524

Scout Association
Baden Powell House, Queen's Gate, London SW7 5JS
Tel. 071 584 7030

Student Christian Movement
186 St Paul's Road, Balsall Heath, Birmingham B12 8LZ
Tel. 021 440 3000

Youth Clubs U.K.
11 St Brides Street, London EC4A 4AS
Tel. 071 353 2366

Youth Exchange Centre
British Council, 10 Spring Gardens, London SW1A 2BN
Tel. 071 389 4030

YMCA
640 Forest Road, London E17 3DZ
Tel. 081 520 5599

YWCA
52 Cornmarket Street, Oxford OX1 3EJ